**Please check all items for damages
before leaving the Library.
Thereafter you will be held
responsible for all injuries
to items beyond reasonable wear.**

Ø 12/14
Ø 4/14

INTRODUCING
ISSUES WITH
OPPOSING
VIEWPOINTS®

Child
Abuse

Jacqueline Langwith, *Book Editor*

GREENHAVEN PRESS
A part of Gale, Cengage Learning

GALE
CENGAGE Learning™

Detroit • New York • San Francisco • New Haven, Conn • Waterville, Maine • London

GALE
CENGAGE Learning

Christine Nasso, *Publisher*
Elizabeth Des Chenes, *Managing Editor*

© 2011 Greenhaven Press, a part of Gale, Cengage Learning

Gale and Greenhaven Press are registered trademarks used herein under license.

For more information, contact:
Greenhaven Press
27500 Drake Rd.
Farmington Hills, MI 48331-3535
Or you can visit our Internet site at gale.cengage.com

For product information and technology assistance, contact us at

Gale Customer Support, 1-800-877-4253
For permission to use material from this text or product, submit all requests online at www.cengage.com/permissions

Further permissions questions can be e-mailed to permissionrequest@cengage.com

Articles in Greenhaven Press anthologies are often edited for length to meet page requirements. In addition, original titles of these works are changed to clearly present the main thesis and to explicitly indicate the author's opinion. Every effort is made to ensure that Greenhaven Press accurately reflects the original intent of the authors. Every effort has been made to trace the owners of copyrighted material.

Cover image copyright © DonSmith/Alamy.

LIBRARY OF CONGRESS CATALOGING-IN-PUBLICATION DATA

Child abuse / Jacqueline Langwith, book editor.
    p. cm. -- (Introducing issues with opposing viewpoints)
  Includes bibliographical references and index.
  ISBN 978-0-7377-5672-2 (hardcover)
  1. Child abuse--United States. 2. Child sexual abuse--United States. 3. Child abuse--United States--Prevention. 4. Child sexual abuse--United States--Prevention.
  I. Langwith, Jacqueline.
   HV6626.52.C5433 2011
   362.7640973--dc22
                                                    2011005625

Printed in the United States of America
  2 3 4 5 6 7 15 14 13 12

Contents

Foreword

I ndulging in a wide spectrum of ideas, beliefs, and perspectives is a critical cornerstone of democracy. After all, it is often debates over differences of opinion, such as whether to legalize abortion, how to treat prisoners, or when to enact the death penalty, that shape our society and drive it forward. Such diversity of thought is frequently regarded as the hallmark of a healthy and civilized culture. As the Reverend Clifford Schutjer of the First Congregational Church in Mansfield, Ohio, declared in a 2001 sermon, "Surrounding oneself with only like-minded people, restricting what we listen to or read only to what we find agreeable is irresponsible. Refusing to entertain doubts once we make up our minds is a subtle but deadly form of arrogance." With this advice in mind, Introducing Issues with Opposing Viewpoints books aim to open readers' minds to the critically divergent views that comprise our world's most important debates.

Introducing Issues with Opposing Viewpoints simplifies for students the enormous and often overwhelming mass of material now available via print and electronic media. Collected in every volume is an array of opinions that captures the essence of a particular controversy or topic. Introducing Issues with Opposing Viewpoints books embody the spirit of nineteenth-century journalist Charles A. Dana's axiom: "Fight for your opinions, but do not believe that they contain the whole truth, or the only truth." Absorbing such contrasting opinions teaches students to analyze the strength of an argument and compare it to its opposition. From this process readers can inform and strengthen their own opinions, or be exposed to new information that will change their minds. Introducing Issues with Opposing Viewpoints is a mosaic of different voices. The authors are statesmen, pundits, academics, journalists, corporations, and ordinary people who have felt compelled to share their experiences and ideas in a public forum. Their words have been collected from newspapers, journals, books, speeches, interviews, and the Internet, the fastest growing body of opinionated material in the world.

Introducing Issues with Opposing Viewpoints shares many of the well-known features of its critically acclaimed parent series, Opposing Viewpoints. The articles are presented in a pro/con format, allowing readers to absorb divergent perspectives side by side. Active reading questions preface each viewpoint, requiring the student to approach the material thoughtfully and carefully. Useful charts, graphs, and cartoons supplement each article. A thorough introduction provides readers with crucial background on an issue. An annotated bibliography points the reader toward articles, books, and websites that contain additional information on the topic. An appendix of organizations to contact contains a wide variety of charities, nonprofit organizations, political groups, and private enterprises that each hold a position on the issue at hand. Finally, a comprehensive index allows readers to locate content quickly and efficiently.

Introducing Issues with Opposing Viewpoints is also significantly different from Opposing Viewpoints. As the series title implies, its presentation will help introduce students to the concept of opposing viewpoints and learn to use this material to aid in critical writing and debate. The series' four-color, accessible format makes the books attractive and inviting to readers of all levels. In addition, each viewpoint has been carefully edited to maximize a reader's understanding of the content. Short but thorough viewpoints capture the essence of an argument. A substantial, thought-provoking essay question placed at the end of each viewpoint asks the student to further investigate the issues raised in the viewpoint, compare and contrast two authors' arguments, or consider how one might go about forming an opinion on the topic at hand. Each viewpoint contains sidebars that include at-a-glance information and handy statistics. A Facts About section located in the back of the book further supplies students with relevant facts and figures.

Following in the tradition of the Opposing Viewpoints series, Greenhaven Press continues to provide readers with invaluable exposure to the controversial issues that shape our world. As John Stuart Mill once wrote: "The only way in which a human being can make some approach to knowing the whole of a subject is by hearing what can be said about it by persons of every variety of opinion and studying all modes in which it can be looked at by every character of mind. No wise man ever acquired his wisdom in any mode but this." It is to this principle that Introducing Issues with Opposing Viewpoints books are dedicated.

Introduction

"Given the known health consequences of a child breathing second-hand smoke, how does the right of the child to good health stack up against the rights of the smoking parents?"

— Elizabeth M. Whelan, president of the American Council on Science and Health

In May 2010 a YouTube video showing a smoking toddler received widespread international attention. The video showed a cute and pudgy two-year-old Indonesian boy, Ardi Rizal, puffing away on a cigarette. News reports said Ardi's father introduced him to smoking when he was eighteen months old and did not see anything wrong with his boy smoking. Child advocates from around the world were outraged and said that Ardi's father should be punished for child abuse because of the harmful effects of smoking on young Ardi's health. There are some people who think that it is child abuse not only to allow children to smoke, but also to expose them to second-hand smoke. They think it should be illegal for parents to smoke around their children, particularly in cars or other enclosed places. There are other people, however, who think that smoking around children is not child abuse and that punishing parents who smoke around their kids is an infringement on their rights.

Secondhand smoke is the smoke that comes out of a smoker's mouth or from the tip of burning cigarettes, pipes, and cigars. Physicians and scientists generally agree that exposure to secondhand smoke is harmful and can lead to a variety of adverse health effects. According to the US Environmental Protection Agency (EPA), secondhand smoke contains hundreds of chemicals known to be toxic or cancer causing.

Children who are exposed to secondhand smoke face more risks from the exposure than adults do. A 2007 report by the US surgeon general revealed that almost 60 percent of US children aged three to eleven are exposed to secondhand smoke. The American Academy of Pediatrics (AAP) claims that the risks these children face because of their exposure include sudden infant death syndrome (SIDS), asthma, ear and respiratory infections, decreased lung growth, and lower capacity for exercise. The AAP says smoking exposure is worse for younger children than older kids and adults, because younger children spend more time in close proximity to parents and have still-developing lungs.

Children with asthma are especially sensitive to secondhand smoke. Secondhand smoke can cause more-frequent asthma attacks, and the attacks may be more severe, requiring trips to the hospital. The California EPA has estimated that secondhand smoke exposure is responsible for 202,300 asthma episodes each year.

Some people believe that because of the harms associated with secondhand smoke, smoking around children constitutes child abuse. In a commentary published in the August 8, 2010, edition of the British newspaper the *Observer*, Steve Fields, the chairman of the Royal College of General Practitioners, declared, "I believe that parents who smoke in cars carrying small children are committing a form of child abuse; I suppose the same people also smoke at home in front of their children." Fields's commentary spurred a great deal of discussion in the United States about whether smoking around children met the legal definition of child abuse.

In the United States, state governments are responsible for enforcing laws against child abuse. Each state provides its own definition of child abuse based on minimum standards set by the federal government. According to federal law, child abuse is defined as an act or a failure to act that presents an imminent risk of serious harm to a child or one that results in death, serious physical or emotional harm, sexual abuse, or exploitation of a child.

On an Internet forum based in Gainesville, Florida, shortly after Fields's commentary was published, moms were discussing whether they felt smoking around children fit the US federal definition of child abuse. One poster, who identified herself as Kathy M., wrote that she believes exposing children to secondhand smoke is child abuse. According to Kathy M., "The children have no say in the damage being done to their bodies, and the parents won't quit unless they are made to quit." She went on to say that exposing children to secondhand smoke fits the federal definition of child abuse because it *immediately* affects the heart and blood circulation in a harmful way, it causes heart disease and lung cancer over the long term, and scientific evidence shows that there is no safe level of exposure to secondhand smoke.

Another mom on the forum with the screen name "LittleMonkeysMom" disagrees with Kathy M. LittleMonkeysMom believes that smoking around children is wrong; however, she does not think it fits the federal definition of child abuse, unless the child exposed to the smoke has asthma. She also thinks telling parents they cannot smoke in their cars would be an infringement on their rights. According to LittleMonkeysMom, "The effects of smoking are not immediate *unless* a child has asthma. . . . I have witnessed pregnant women smoking, new parents holding their baby and smoking, children in cars with people smoking (windows down of course) and what can you really do without causing a scene? To tell people that they cannot smoke in their cars would be considered against their rights."

Kathy M.'s opinion is shared by Michael Siegel, a professor at Boston University School of Public Health and the creator of a tobacco news and analysis blog called *The Rest of the Story*. Siegel believes that there is a difference between causing harm and increasing risk, and while smoking may increase risk, it does not cause immediate harm. He compares smoking to a number of other behaviors that parents do—or allow their children to do—that are risky but are not considered child abuse. On his December 10, 2007, blog, Siegel posted the following:

> Feeding a child large portions of high-fat, greasy foods increases the child's risk of developing adverse health outcomes, such as obesity. . . . Feeding a child large quantities of food containing trans-fats increases the risk for later cardiovascular disease. Allowing a child to play hockey increases that child's risk for severe head and neck injuries. Allowing a child to ride in a lawn tractor greatly increases the child's risk for loss of limbs. But none of these behaviors are considered to be child abuse because they only increase risk. They do not directly and necessarily cause harm to the child.

Siegel believes that exposing children to secondhand smoke may increase a child's risk of certain health problems, but it does not immediately cause harm. Therefore it is not child abuse. Like

LittleMonkeysMom, however, Siegel does believe that smoking around children with asthma may qualify as child abuse.

Some states already have laws banning smoking around children in certain instances, but they stop short of calling it child abuse. In Arkansas, California, Louisiana, Maine, and Oregon, it is illegal to smoke in cars when children are present. California's law bans smoking in cars when there are children aged seventeen and younger present and charges those caught violating the law with up to a one-hundred-dollar fine. David Schapira, a former state representative from Arizona, tried to enact legislation that would make smoking in a vehicle with anyone seventeen and younger a crime in his state. The legislation he sponsored did not become a law, but it would have allowed the police to pull drivers over and charge fines of fifty dollars or more per child. In a story in the *Arizona Review* in 2007, Schapira said, "We already protect children from child abuse. . . . I think if you are smoking in a vehicle . . . to me that is child abuse." In states where it is illegal to smoke in cars with children, parents are subject to traffic penalties. They are not charged with child abuse, however.

While a handful of states ban smoking in cars with children, many more states prohibit smoking in foster care homes and consider parental smoking in custody cases. Alaska, Arizona, Maine, Montana, New Jersey, North Dakota, Oklahoma, Oregon, Texas, Vermont, and Washington have all passed laws or regulations to protect foster children from secondhand smoke. At least fifteen states, including Florida, Illinois, Maryland, Massachusetts, Michigan, and Pennsylvania, allow judges to consider parental smoking as a means of determining which parent gets custody in divorce cases.

Whether smoking around children is considered child abuse, or some other type of crime is just one of the many debates concerning the abuse and neglect of children. In *Introducing Issues with Opposing Viewpoints: Child Abuse*, the contributors debate many other issues in the following chapters: How Serious Is the Problem of Child Abuse? What Are the Causes of Child Abuse? and What Is the Best Way to Prevent Child Abuse?

Chapter 1

How Serious Is the Problem of Child Abuse?

The definition of child abuse in the United States may depend on the state in which the abuse occurs.

There Is a Child Abuse Crisis in America

Marian Wright Edelman

"The statistics are shocking: A child is abused or neglected every 40 seconds."

In the following viewpoint, Marian Wright Edelman asserts that there is a child abuse and neglect crisis in America. Edelman says the consequences of child abuse are tragic. Child abuse and neglect result in the deaths of many innocent children in America, she says. Those who survive through childhood are haunted by problems, such as drug abuse and promiscuity, as adults. Edelman believes family- and parent-oriented prevention programs offer a promising approach for helping to decrease the level of child abuse in America. Edelman is the president and founder of the Children's Defense Fund, a nonprofit organization devoted to children.

AS YOU READ, CONSIDER THE FOLLOWING QUESTIONS:

1. According to Edelman, how many maltreated children receive services after an initial investigation of child abuse?
2. According to a study by the US Centers for Disease Control and Prevention, a certain prevention program was able to reduce child abuse rates in the communities where it was available. What is the name of the program, according to Edelman?
3. What is the name of the law enacted by the 110th US Congress that Edelman thinks will help abused and neglected children?

Marian Wright Edelman, "National Child Abuse Prevention Month," *Child Watch Columns*, April 17, 2009. Reproduced by permission.

April is National Child Abuse Prevention Month—a good time for us to look at the child abuse and neglect crisis in America. The statistics are shocking: A child is abused or neglected every 40 seconds. During 2007, an estimated 794,000 children were determined to be victims of child abuse or neglect, and almost 3.2 million children were subjects of abuse or neglect investigations. Nearly 60 percent of child victims suffered from neglect, the most common form of child maltreatment. These include some of our youngest children. Almost 22 of every 1,000 children under the age of one were victims of child abuse or neglect.

The Consequences of Child Abuse

Too few abused and neglected children get the help they need. Only slightly more than 60 percent of maltreated children received any services after an initial investigation. The consequences are deadly: 1,760 children died from abuse and neglect in 2007—nearly five children a day.

Not only is child maltreatment cruel and wrong, it also carries a heavy economic cost. Prevent Child Abuse America, a national

Not enough abused children get the help they need. Almost 40 percent of maltreated children do not receive any help or services after an initial investigation.

organization that builds awareness about this issue, estimates that the direct and indirect costs of abuse and neglect to the United States are more than $284 million every day, nearly $104 billion each year. Child maltreatment and repeated exposure to domestic violence have been associated with negative behaviors and poor health outcomes in adulthood. Studies have found that toxic stress in children can result in alcoholism, drug abuse, eating disorders, promiscuity, smoking and suicide later in life.

But nine times more federal child welfare dollars are spent on out-of-home care for victims of abuse or neglect than on preventive services. Focusing on prevention is crucial, especially during an economic downturn. The added stress on families can result in increased reports of child abuse and neglect. Recent media reports show that this is already beginning to happen in communities across the country.

Successful Prevention Programs

What can we do to prevent child abuse and neglect from starting or recurring? There are solutions that work. Studies have shown home visiting and other family support programs can help prevent child maltreatment. One recent study funded by the Centers for Disease Control and Prevention found that communities where the Positive Parenting Program was available to all parents had significantly lower rates of confirmed child abuse, fewer placements into foster care, and fewer hospitalizations from child abuse injuries when compared to communities without access to the program. A study of the Nurse Family Partnership Program showed that unmarried and low-income women and their very young children who received regular home visits from nurses had 48 percent fewer verified reports of child abuse or neglect. Another study demonstrated that Healthy Families, another home visiting program, reduced abuse and neglect of young children.

> **FAST FACT**
>
> According to the US Department of Health and Human Services, studies in Nevada and Colorado estimate that as many as 50 percent to 60 percent of child deaths resulting from abuse or neglect are not recorded as such.

Number of Child Deaths per Day Due to Child Maltreatment in America

Year	Deaths per Day
1996	2.56
1997	2.68
1998	3.01
1999	2.98
2000	3.58
2001	3.76
2002	3.45
2003	3.22
2004	3.95
2005	3.87
2006	3.78
2007	4.38
2008	4.47

Taken from: US Department of Health and Human Services, Administration for Children & Families, "Statistics and Research: Child Abuse & Neglect Research." www.acf.hhs.gov/programs/cb/stats_research/index.htm.

Programs that identify families who may need support early and provide help as soon as problems begin also are effective. A number of states are implementing new response systems as alternatives to the routine child abuse or neglect investigation process to help families receive support sooner. Some states are finding new ways to evaluate families' strengths and needs and bring together extended family and others to assist overwhelmed parents. Children in foster care who have been abused or neglected often need special support. A new law enacted in the 110th Congress [2007–2008], the Fostering Connections to Success and Increasing Adoptions Act, will help these children get the education, health care and permanence they need in their lives. This new act now needs to be implemented across the country to truly benefit children.

We need to increase states' and communities' ability to address substance abuse, mental health problems and domestic violence—problems that bring children to the attention of the child welfare system. Evidence shows that comprehensive family-based treatment works; family drug courts can be effective; treatment for mothers who are depressed or have other mental health problems helps them meet the needs of their children. We must support agencies offering critical family assistance or treatment services to children and families in crisis.

Everybody's Business

Preventing child abuse and neglect is everybody's business—not a job for government alone. Many improvements are needed in the way public agencies respond to child maltreatment. But all of us can make a difference. Reach out to an overwhelmed parent with young children. Volunteer at a public agency serving families in crisis. National Child Abuse Prevention Month is a time to commit to working together as parents, grandparents, aunts, uncles, teachers, coaches, faith leaders, staff of protective service agencies and programs, and policy makers to keep our children safe.

EVALUATING THE AUTHOR'S ARGUMENTS:

Marian Wright Edelman used some statistics in her viewpoint. Do you think she made good use of statistics in making her point that there is a child abuse crisis in America? Explain.

Child Abuse Is Decreasing in America

David Crary

"There's much more public awareness and public intolerance around child abuse now."

In the following viewpoint David Crary asserts that child abuse in America has declined steeply. Crary bases his assertion on the Fourth National Incidence Study of Child Abuse and Neglect (NIS-4), performed by the US Department of Health and Human Services. The study found that child abuse rates dropped between 1993 and 2005–2006. According to Crary, experts think the declines in child abuse and neglect are due to greater public awareness and more people working to keep kids safe. Crary, who covers family and relationship issues, is an acclaimed journalist for the Associated Press.

AS YOU READ, CONSIDER THE FOLLOWING QUESTIONS:

1. According to Crary, the fourth installment of the National Incidence Study of Child Abuse and Neglect (NIS-4) is based on information from 10,700 sentinels. Who are these sentinels?
2. What does Crary say is "one curious aspect" of the NIS-4 study?
3. According to the cited NIS-4 study, poor children were how many times more likely than other kids to experience abuse?

NEW YORK—A massive new federal study documents an unprecedented and dramatic decrease in incidents of serious child abuse, especially sexual abuse. Experts hailed the findings as proof that crackdowns and public-awareness campaigns had made headway.

An estimated 553,000 children suffered physical, sexual or emotional abuse in 2005–06, down 26 percent from the estimated 743,200 abuse victims in 1993, the study found.

"It's the first time since we started collecting data about these things that we've seen substantial declines over a long period, and that's tremendously encouraging," said professor David Finkelhor of the University of New Hampshire, a leading researcher in the field of child abuse.

"It does suggest that the mobilization around this issue is helping and it's a problem that is amenable to solutions," he said.

The findings were contained in the fourth installment of the National Incidence Study of Child Abuse and Neglect, a congressionally mandated study that has been conducted periodically by the Department of Health and Human Services. The previous version was issued in 1996, based on 1993 data.

FAST FACT

In 2005–2006, one in every fifty-eight children experienced maltreatment. This was fewer than in 1993, when one child in every forty-three suffered maltreatment, according to the third and fourth installments of the National Incidence Study of Child Abuse and Neglect in the United States.

The new study is based on information from more than 10,700 "sentinels"—such as child-welfare workers, police officers, teachers, health care professionals and day care workers—in 122 counties nationwide. The detailed data collected from them was then used to make national estimates.

The number of sexually abused children decreased from 217,700 in 1993 to 135,300 in 2005-06—a 38 percent drop, the study shows.

The number of children who experienced physical abuse fell by 15 percent, and the number of emotionally abused children dropped by 27 percent.

Rates of Abuse and Neglect Are in Decline

The US Department of Health and Human Services has definitional standards for harm. In order to be counted in the Fourth National Incidence Study of Child Abuse and Neglect, children must have experienced observable harm or injury at the hands of a person responsible for their care.

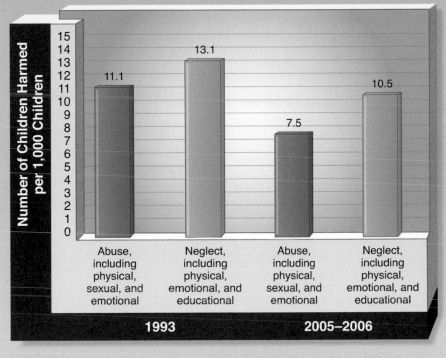

Taken from: US Department of Health and Human Services, Fourth National Incidence Study of Child Abuse and Neglect (NIS-4), January 2010.

The 455-page study shied away from trying to explain the trends, but other experts weighed in.

"There's much more public awareness and public intolerance around child abuse now," said Linda Spears, the Child Welfare League of America's vice president for public policy. "It was a hidden concern before—people were afraid to talk about it if it was in their family."

She also noted the proliferation of programs designed to help abusers and potential abusers overcome their problems.

Finkelhor, whose own previous research detected a drop in abuse rates, said the study reveals "real, substantial declines" that cannot be

Kathie Lee Gifford helps promote the nationwide hammocks campaign in support of the leading child abuse charity, Childhelp. The author believes that the growing number of child abuse awareness and support groups has contributed to the decline in incidences of child abuse.

dismissed on any technical grounds, such as changing definitions of abuse.

Increase in Arrests

He suggested that the decline was a product of several coinciding trends, including a "troop surge" in the 1990s when more people were deployed in child-protection services and the criminal-justice system intensified its anti-abuse efforts with more arrests and prison sentences.

Finkelhor also suggested that the greatly expanded use of medications may have enabled many potential child abusers to treat the conditions that otherwise might have led them to molest or mistreat a child.

"There's also been a general change in perceptions and norms about what one can get away with, so much more publicity about these things," he said.

One curious aspect of the study was the manner of its release.

Although HHS had launched the study in 2004 and invested several million dollars, it was posted a few days ago on the Internet with no fanfare—neither a media release nor a news conference.

Poor Kids at Higher Risk

The findings might be disconcerting to some in the child-welfare field who base their funding pitches on the specter of ever-rising abuse rates, said Richard Wexler, executive director of the National Coalition for Child Protection Reform.

"The best use of scarce child-welfare dollars is on prevention and family preservation—not on hiring more people to investigate less actual abuse," Wexler said.

The study found some dramatic differences in child-abuse rates based on socio-economic factors. Poor children were three times more likely than other kids to experience abuse, and rates of abuse in African-American families were significantly higher than for whites and Latinos.

Family structure also was a factor. For example, children with a single parent who had a live-in partner faced an abuse rate 10 times that of a child living with two parents.

The main author of the study, Andrea Sedlak of the Rockville, Md.–based research firm Westat Inc., said she was heartened by the overall findings of declining abuse rates. However, she was troubled to find that more than half of child-maltreatment incidents are not investigated by child-protection agencies.

"Is the system still so strapped?" she asked. "There's still a lot of material here saying the system has a long way to go."

EVALUATING THE AUTHORS' ARGUMENTS:

After reading this viewpoint by David Crary and the previous viewpoint by Marian Wright Edelman, are you heartened or discouraged by the level of child abuse in America? Explain.

Child Sexual Abuse Is a Crisis in the Catholic Church

"It's ... about indulgence— the institutional indulgence, fitful but systemic, of the sexual exploitation of children by priests."

Hendrik Hertzberg

The sexual exploitation of children by priests is a widespread problem in the Catholic Church, contends Hendrik Hertzberg in the following viewpoint. He says allegations of abuse against priests are surfacing in a growing list of countries, suggesting that the problem is systemic in the church. Hertzberg thinks the institutional structure of the church makes it difficult for the pope and other Catholic leaders to come to terms with and respond properly to the crisis. Hertzberg is a senior editor and staff writer at *The New Yorker*.

AS YOU READ, CONSIDER THE FOLLOWING QUESTIONS:

1. According to Hertzberg, who said, "The current revelations of abuse are the tip of an iceberg"?
2. With whom did the pope meet during his 2008 visit to the United States, according to Hertzberg?
3. What does the author say are the political structures the Catholic Church is modeled on?

On October 31, 1517, a Roman Catholic priest and theologian, Dr. Martin Luther, put the finishing touches on a series of bullet points and, legend has it, nailed the result to the door of the castle church in Wittenberg, Germany—the equivalent, for the time and place, of uploading a particularly explosive blog post. Luther's was a protest against the sale of chits that were claimed to entitle buyers or their designees to shorter stays in Purgatory. Such chits, known as indulgences, were being hawked as part of Pope Leo X's fund-raising drive for the renovation of St. Peter's Basilica. The "Ninety-five Theses on the Power and Efficacy of Indulgences" touched off a high-stakes flame war that rapidly devolved into the real thing, with actual wars, actual flames, and actual stakes. The theological clash that sundered Christendom didn't just change the face of Western religion; it birthed the modern world.

Half a millennium later, the present agony of Catholicism is very far from being in the same league, even though the *National Catholic Reporter* has called it "the largest institutional crisis in centuries, possibly in Church history." The crisis is not about doctrine, at least not directly. It's about administration; it's about the structure of power within the Catholic Church; it's about the Church's insular, self-protective clerical culture. And, of course, like nearly every one of the controversies that preoccupy and bedevil the Church—abortion, stem-cell research, contraception, celibacy, marriage and divorce and affectional orientation—it's about sex.

It's also about indulgence—the institutional indulgence, fitful but systemic, of the sexual exploitation of children by priests. The pattern broke into public consciousness in the United States a quarter of a century ago, when a Louisiana priest pleaded guilty to thirty-three counts of crimes against children and was sentenced to prison. Since then, there have been thousands of such cases, civil and criminal, involving many thousands of children and leading to legal settlements that have amounted to more than two billion dollars and have driven several dioceses into bankruptcy. In 1992, Richard Sipe, a Catholic psychotherapist and researcher who served for eighteen years as a priest and Benedictine monk, told a conference of victims that "the current revelations of abuse are the tip of an iceberg, and if the problem is traced to its foundations the path will lead to the highest halls of the Vatican."

America's liberal system of tort law, along with the enterprising reporting of journalists at newspapers like the Boston *Globe*, brought the problem to light earlier here than elsewhere. But it can no longer be dismissed as an epiphenomenon of America's sexual libertinism and religious indiscipline. In Ireland, for example, where Church-run orphanages and other institutions for children are supported by the state, a government commission reported last year that

> the Dublin Archdiocese's preoccupations in dealing with cases of child sexual abuse, at least until the mid 1990s, were the maintenance of secrecy, the avoidance of scandal, the protection of the reputation of the Church, and the preservation of its assets. All other considerations, including the welfare of children and justice for victims, were subordinated to these priorities.

The past few years have seen a cascade of revelations from many countries, including, most recently, Germany, and in the past month the cascade has become a flood. Sipe's prediction has come true. As Cardinal Archbishop of Munich, as Prefect of the Congregation for the Doctrine of the Faith, and now as Pope Benedict XVI, Joseph Ratzinger appears to have been at best neglectful, at worst complicit, in minimizing and covering up specific cases of abuse that came under his supervision.

FAST FACT

According to the 2004 John Jay report, commissioned by the US Conference of Catholic Bishops, 4,392 priests and deacons in the United States were accused of child sexual abuse.

The response of the ecclesiastical powers that be, once outright denial became untenable, has all along been an unsatisfactory mixture of contrition and irritation. From Benedict on down, Church fathers have made statements of apology and shame. Awareness programs have been launched, studies have been conducted, bishops have been obliged to resign. The Pope met personally with victims of abuse during his visit to the United States, in 2008, and even his critics agree that he has taken the problem more seriously, both before and since his elevation to the throne of St. Peter, than did his predecessor, the soon-to-be-sainted John Paul II.

According to the author, reaction to Pope Benedict XVI's response to the sexual exploitation of children by Catholic priests has been highly charged. Supporters argue that he has taken the problem more seriously than previous popes, while critics say his response has been one of neglect—and possibly complicity.

On the other hand, that's not setting the bar very high. When serious discipline has been imposed, it has generally been in the wake of bad publicity, usually from outside the Church and always from outside the hierarchy. There has been a lot of bad publicity of late, and some of the reaction has been tinged with resentful paranoia. In an editorial, *L'Osservatore Romano*, the official Vatican newspaper, accused "the media" of having the "rather obvious and ignoble intention of attacking Benedict XVI and his closest collaborators at all costs." This was echoed, nearer home, by the Archbishop of New York, Timothy Dolan, who, in his blog (yes, he has one), accused the *Times* of "being part of a well-oiled campaign against Pope Benedict." Back in Rome, on Palm Sunday, the Pope himself spoke darkly of "the petty gossip of dominant opinion."

The Catholic Church is an authoritarian institution, modelled on the political structures of the Roman Empire and medieval Europe. It is better at transmitting instructions downward than at facilitating accountability upward. It is monolithic. It claims the unique legitimacy of a line of succession going back to the apostolic circle of Jesus Christ. Its leaders are protected by a nimbus of mystery, pomp, holiness, and, in the case of the Pope, infallibility—to be sure, only in certain doctrinal matters, not administrative ones, but the aura is not so selective. The hierarchy of such an institution naturally resists admitting to moral turpitude and sees squalid scandal as a mortal threat. Equally important, the government of the Church is entirely male.

It is not "anti-Catholic" to hypothesize that these things may have something to do with the Church's extraordinary difficulty in coming to terms with clerical sexual abuse. The iniquities now roiling the Catholic Church are more shocking than the ones that so outraged Martin Luther. But the broader society in which the Church is embedded has grown incomparably freer. To the extent that the Church manages to purge itself of its shame—its sins, its crimes—it will owe a debt of gratitude to the lawyers, the journalists, and, above all, the victims and families who have had the courage to persevere, against formidable resistance, in holding it to account. Without their efforts, the suffering of tens of thousands of children would still be a secret. Our largely democratic, secularist, liberal, pluralist modern world, against which the Church has so often set its face, turns out to be its best teacher—and the savior, you might say, of its most vulnerable, most trusting communicants.

EVALUATING THE AUTHOR'S ARGUMENTS:

Hendrik Hetzberg believes that child sexual exploitation is a crisis in the Catholic Church. What factors in the church does Hertzberg blame for causing the crisis?

Child Sexual Abuse in the Catholic Church Is No Worse Than in the Rest of the World

"Your child is less likely to be abused by a Catholic or Anglican priest in the west today than by the members of almost any other profession."

Andrew Brown

In the following viewpoint Andrew Brown contends that the frequency of child sexual abuse in the Catholic Church is not any different than that in the wider world, although boys are more likely to be victims in the Catholic Church than are girls. Brown believes the world's focus on church abuse makes it seem worse than in the rest of the world. He asserts that children are more likely to be abused by those in other professions or at the hands of a family member than by a priest. Brown has authored several books and blogs for *The Guardian*, a British newspaper.

AS YOU READ, CONSIDER THE FOLLOWING QUESTIONS:
  1. What does Brown say is the pattern of victimization among American Catholic priests?
  2. How many children are reported to social services in Sweden every year, according to Camila Batmanghelidjh?
  3. Why does Brown believe the Roman Catholic Church has a tendency to cover up institutional wrongdoing?

M any Catholic priests and religious have abused children in their care. But is the church's record worse than the world's?

There seems to be no end to the scandals buffeting the Roman Catholic church about the abuse of children; most recently in Germany, where the headmaster at a school associated with a choir once run by the pope's elder brother Georg Ratzinger has been exposed as an abuser. And there is no doubt that a lot of children were damaged for life by priests, and that this was mostly covered up by the hierarchy until recently. But was the Catholic church unfairly singled out? Aren't all children vulnerable to exploitation, especially when they are poor and unwanted?

FAST FACT

According to the sixth annual report on implementation of the "Charter for the Protection of Children and Young People," US dioceses and religious orders spent more than $436 million in 2008 on settlements and other costs related to clergy sex abuse, a decrease of 29 percent over the $615 million paid out in the peak year of 2007.

The Unique Pattern of Catholic Child Abuse

These questions lead into a thicket of horror. The most detailed statistics on child abuse for the Catholic clergy that I can find come from the John Jay Institute's report drawn up for the American Catholic bishops' conference. From this it emerges that the frequency of child abuse among Catholic priests is not remarkable but its pattern is. Although there are no figures for the number of abusers in the wider population, there are figures for the number of victims. These vary wildly: the most pessimistic survey finds that 27% of American women and 16% of men had "a history of childhood sexual abuse"; while the the most optimistic had 12.8% of women and 4.3% of men. Obviously a great deal depends here on the definition of abuse; also on the definition of "childhood". In some of these surveys it runs up to [the age of] 18. . . .

The Catholic figures show that between about 4% of priests and deacons serving in the US between 1950 and 2002 had been accused of sexual abuse of someone under 18. In this country [United Kingdom] the figure was a 10th of that: 0.4% But whereas the victims in the general population are overwhelmingly female, the pattern among American Catholic priests was quite different. Four out of five of their victims were male. Most were adolescents: two out of five were 14 or over; 15% were under 10.

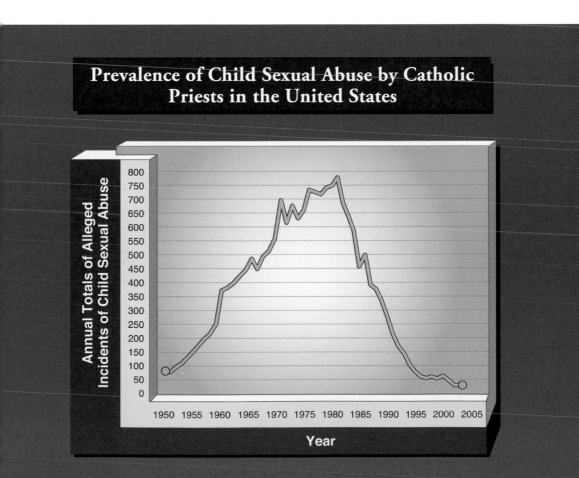

Prevalence of Child Sexual Abuse by Catholic Priests in the United States

Annual Totals of Alleged Incidents of Child Sexual Abuse

Year

Taken from: John Jay College of Criminal Justice, "The Nature and Scope of the Problem of Sexual Abuse of Minors by Catholic Priests and Deacons in the United States," 2004.

This is vile, but whether it is more vile than the record of any other profession is not obvious. The concentration on boys makes the Catholic pattern of abuse stand out; what makes it so shocking is that parents trusted their children with priests. They stood in for the parents. But this isn't all that different from the pattern in the wider world, either, where the vast majority of abuse comes from within families. The other point that makes the Catholic abuse [stand out] is that it is nowadays very widely reported. It may be the best reported crime in the world: that, too, tends to skew perceptions.

There are, however, some fragments of figures from the outside world suggesting that not many professions do better. Last year [in 2009] it was reported that half of the girls fostered in social democratic Sweden in the 50s and 60s had been abused; according to [child

Prior to a Catholic mass in Dublin, a survivor of clerical abuse confronts Archbishop Diarmuid Martin. The Catholic priest child abuse scandal was perhaps most damaging to the church in Ireland.

advocate] Camila Batmanghelidjh 550,000 children are reported to the social services in this country every year.

Cover-Up Draws Attention

So why the concentration on Catholic priests and brothers? Perhaps I am unduly cynical, but I believe that all institutions attempt to cover up institutional wrongdoing although the Roman Catholic church has had a higher opinion of itself than most, and thus a greater tendency to lie about these things. Because it is an extremely authoritarian institution at least within the hierarchy, it is also one where there were few checks and balances on the misbehaviour of the powerful. The scandal has been loudest and most damaging in Ireland, because it came along just at the moment when the church was losing its power over society at large, and where it was no longer able to cover up what had happened, but still willing to try. Much the same is true in the diocese of Boston which was bankrupted by the scandal.

It doesn't seem to be true, though, that this was a problem spread by Irish priests around the world, as some traditionalists have argued. Certainly, the geographical spread across the US was fairly even, and not concentrated in areas of high Irish settlement and tradition. But in Ireland the state was happy to hand over the problem of unwanted children to the church.

Certainly the safeguards against paedophilia in the priesthood are now among the tightest in the world. That won't stop a steady trickle of scandals; but I think that objectively your child is less likely to be abused by a Catholic or Anglican priest in the west today than by the members of almost any other profession.

> ### EVALUATING THE AUTHORS' ARGUMENTS:
>
> Despite their opposing viewpoints, there are certain things that Andrew Brown and the author of the previous viewpoint, Hendrik Hertzberg, seem to agree upon. In what ways do they agree?

"Thousands of children are raped and molested every year while in the government's care—most often, by the very corrections officials charged with their rehabilitation and protection."

There Is a Child Sexual Abuse Epidemic in Juvenile Prisons

David Kaiser and Lovisa Stannow

Every year thousands of youths in American juvenile detention facilities are sexually abused, argue David Kaiser and Lovisa Stannow in the following viewpoint. According to Kaiser and Stannow, a 2010 report issued by the US Bureau of Justice reveals a hidden abuse epidemic going on in juvenile prisons. Youths, many incarcerated for nonviolent offenses like truancy or running away, are repeatedly abused by staff and other prisoners, maintain the authors. The majority of abusers are prison staff. Yet, say the authors, they are rarely punished. Kaiser and Stannow are with the human rights organization Just Detention International, which seeks to end sexual abuse in detention.

W hen Troy Erik Isaac was first imprisoned in California, his cellmate made the introductions for both of them. "He said to me, 'Your name is gonna be Baby Romeo, and I'm Big Romeo.' He was saying he would be my man." Troy was twelve at the time. A skinny, terrified little kid, he accepted the prisoner's bargain being imposed on him: protection for sex. He wasn't protected, though. Soon he was attacked and raped at night by another cellmate, a sixteen-year-old. He told staff he was suicidal, hoping to be placed in solitary confinement, but they ignored him; the rapes continued.

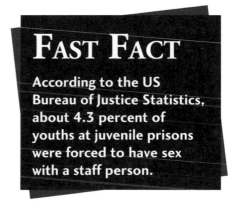

FAST FACT

According to the US Bureau of Justice Statistics, about 4.3 percent of youths at juvenile prisons were forced to have sex with a staff person.

In 2005, the Department of Justice investigated a juvenile facility in Plainfield, Indiana, where kids sexually abused one another so often and in such numbers that staff created flow charts to track the incidents. Investigators found "youths weighing under 70 pounds who engaged in sexual acts with youths who weighed as much as 100 pounds more than them."

Reporters in Texas, in 2007, discovered that more than 750 juvenile detainees across the state had alleged sexual abuse by staff over the previous six years. That number, however, was generally thought to under-represent the true extent of such abuse, because most children were too afraid to report it: staff commonly instructed their favorite inmates to beat up kids who complained. Even when the kids did file complaints, they knew it wouldn't do them much good. Staff covered for each other, grievance processes were sabotaged and evidence was frequently destroyed. Officials in Austin ignored what they heard, and in the very rare instances when staff were fired and their cases referred to local prosecutors, those prosecutors usually refused to act. Not one employee of the Texas Youth Commission during that six-year period was sent to prison for raping the children in his or her care.

Abuse Is Widespread

Until now, when such stories have made it into the press, officials have been able to contend that they reflected anomalous failings of a particular facility or system. But a report released this morning [January 7, 2010] by the Bureau of Justice Statistics (BJS) should change that. Mandated by the Prison Rape Elimination Act of 2003 (PREA), and easily the largest and most authoritative study of the problem ever conducted, it makes clear that sexual abuse in juvenile detention is a national crisis.

This is a difficult problem to measure, since some inmates make false claims, and some, fearing retaliation even when promised anonymity, choose not to report abuse. Overall, most experts believe that the numbers such studies produce are usually too low. But 12.1 percent of kids taking the BJS survey across the country said they'd been sexually abused at their current facility during the preceding year. That's approximately 3,220 out of the 26,550 who were eligible to take it.

The survey, however, was given only at large facilities that held youth that have been tried for some offense for at least ninety days. That's more restrictive than it may sound. In total, according to the most recent data, there are nearly 93,000 kids in juvenile detention on any given day. Although we can't assume that 12.1 percent of the larger number were sexually abused—many kids not covered by the survey are held for short periods of time, or in small facilities where rates of abuse are somewhat lower—we can say confidently that the BJS's 3,320 figure represents only a small fraction of the juveniles sexually abused in detention every year.

What sort of kids get locked up in the first place? Only 34 percent of those in juvenile detention are there for violent crimes. (More than

President George W. Bush signs the Prison Rape Elimination Act of 2003. The legislation created a national commission to examine the impact of prison rape on its victims and the country's correctional system.

200,000 youth are also tried as adults in the U.S. every year, and on any given day approximately 8,500 kids under 18 are confined in adult prisons and jails. Although probably at greater risk of sexual abuse than any other detained population, they weren't included in the BJS study.) According to a report by the National Prison Rape Elimination Commission, which was itself created by PREA, more than 20 percent of those in juvenile detention were confined for technical offenses such as violating probation, or for "status offenses" like disobeying parental orders, missing curfews, truancy, or running away—often from violence and abuse at home. Many suffer from mental illness, substance abuse, and learning disabilities.

A Staff Problem

A full 80 percent of the abuse reported in the study was perpetrated not by other inmates but by staff. And shockingly, 95 percent of the youth making such allegations said they were victimized by female staff. 63 percent of them reported at least one incident of sexual

Juvenile Prisoners Are Abused at a Higher Rate Than Adult Prisoners

One in every twenty people in prison was sexually assaulted in 2009.

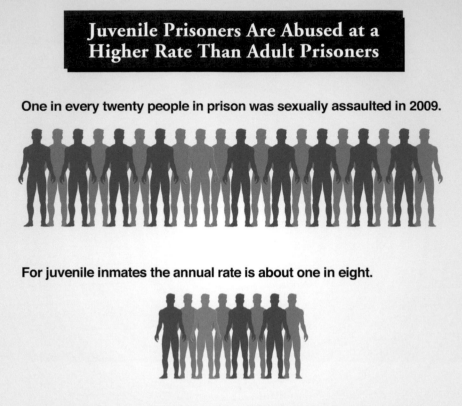

For juvenile inmates the annual rate is about one in eight.

Taken from: Michelle Chen, "Groups Press Justice Department on Prison Rape," August 18, 2010. http://colorlines.com.

contact with staff in which no force or explicit coercion was used; staff caught having sex with inmates often claim it's consensual. But staff have enormous control over inmates' lives. They can give them privileges, such as extra food or clothing or the opportunity to wash, and they can punish them: everything from beatings to solitary confinement to extended sentences. The notion of a truly consensual relationship in such circumstances is grotesque even when the inmate is not a child.

Nationally, however, fewer than half of the corrections officials whose sexual abuse of juveniles is confirmed are referred for prosecution, and almost none are seriously punished. Although it is a crime for staff to have sex with inmates in all 50 states, prosecutors rarely take on such cases. As children's advocate Isela Gutierrez put it to *The Texas Observer*, "Local prosecutors don't consider these kids to be their constituents." A quarter of all known staff predators in youth facilities are allowed to keep their positions.

The biggest risk factor found in the study was prior abuse. 65 percent of those who had previously been sexually assaulted at another correctional facility were also assaulted at their current one. In prison culture, even in juvenile detention, after an inmate is raped for the first time he is considered "turned out," and fair game for further abuse. 81 percent of those sexually abused by other inmates were victimized more than once, and 32 percent more than ten times. 42 percent were assaulted by more than one perpetrator. Of those victimized by staff, 88 percent had been abused repeatedly, 27 percent more than ten times, and 33 percent by more than one facility employee. Those who took the survey had been in their facilities for an average of just half a year. In essence, the survey shows that thousands of children are raped and molested every year while in the government's care—most often, by the very corrections officials charged with their rehabilitation and protection.

Reform Is Slow to Occur

The necessary precautions to prevent this horrific treatment are clear. So far, however, reform has been slow. The Plainfield unit was converted to an adult facility after the Department of Justice investigation; nonetheless, two other juvenile facilities in Indiana were on the BJS report's list of the thirteen worst nationally, as were two in Texas. In 2005, The Department of Justice investigated the L.E. Rader Center in Oklahoma. Although the state Attorney General's office "refused to allow the United States the opportunity to tour the Rader facility," investigators examining documents discovered, among other problems, rampant sexual abuse of the facility's boys by female staff. It concluded that Oklahoma "fails to protect youth confined at Rader from harm due to constitutionally deficient practices." But years later, Rader too is on the BJS's list of worst facilities: 25 percent of its inmates still claim abuse by staff.

A recommendation by the Office of Children and Family Services (OCFS) in New York that judges avoid sentencing children to the state's juvenile detention facilities unless they pose a significant risk to public safety has received a great deal of press. . . . That recommendation followed multiple revelations of violent, neglectful, and abusive conditions—first in a Human Rights Watch report issued in 2006, then in a 2009 Department of Justice investigation, and finally in the report of a taskforce created by Governor [David] Paterson. Most of the abuses described in these documents were not sexual. Now, though, we are told that the problems in New York are even worse than reported. New York juvenile facilities surveyed by the BJS did not in aggregate perform markedly better than the national average. It turns out that sexual abuse is yet another crisis in the state's juvenile detention system, as it is across the country.

EVALUATING THE AUTHORS' ARGUMENTS:

In this viewpoint David Kaiser and Lovisa Stannow argue that there is an epidemic of sexual abuse at juvenile detention facilities. Do the authors provide any recommendations on how to address the problem? If so, what do you think of their recommendations? If not, why do you think they chose not to?

Malicious Child Poisoning Is a Serious Problem

JoNel Aleccia

"We believe that the malicious use of pharmaceuticals may be an under-recognized form and/ or component of child maltreatment."

In the following viewpoint JoNel Aleccia asserts that there is a hidden problem in America of parents and childcare givers poisoning children with drugs. Aleccia discusses a study that analyzes incidents from the National Poison Data System. The study found that between 2000 and 2008, thousands of children were maliciously poisoned with drugs and alcohol. According to the author, researchers do not understand the motives behind the child poisonings. Aleccia is a health writer for MSNBC.com.

AS YOU READ, CONSIDER THE FOLLOWING QUESTIONS:

1. Shan Yin, leader of the child poisoning study discussed in this viewpoint, analyzed cases of drug and alcohol poisoning from the National Poison Data System coded as what?
2. Do poison center records include motives for the child poisonings?
3. What does Yin say he hopes his study will make people give more consideration to?

Parents and caregivers who slip young, healthy children doses of common drugs—including painkillers, sedatives and laxatives—are fueling a dangerous but hidden form of child abuse, new research finds.

About 160 kids are hurt in the United States each year—and at least two die—after being forced to ingest antidepressants, cough and cold medicines, even drugs to treat high blood pressure. Many are given alcohol, marijuana or cocaine, according to the first large-scale study of the issue published in the *Journal of Pediatrics*.

"We believe that the malicious use of pharmaceuticals may be an under-recognized form and/or component of child maltreatment," said Dr. Shan Yin, who led the study conducted at the Rocky Mountain Poison and Drug Center in Denver.

Yin, a medical toxicologist, analyzed more than 21.4 million calls to the National Poison Data System between 2000 and 2008. When he looked at cases of drug and alcohol poisoning coded as "malicious" in children younger than 7, Shin found 1,439 cases of kids who'd been exposed. Some 172 children were seriously injured and 18 died.

They included a 4-month-old girl killed in 2003 when a babysitter gave her a full bottle of decongestant, and a 5-year-old girl who died in 2006 after her mother gave her antidepressants and muscle relaxants.

"I just don't know what goes on in the minds of people who try to harm their child," said Yin, an emergency room doctor who has treated cases of abuse.

Parents May Be Angry, Frustrated

Poison center records don't include motives for the poisonings, said Yin. But he speculates that known causes for child abuse—punishment, frustration with the demands of parenting—may play a role in drug-induced harm.

"There's a very wide spectrum, from frank homicides to people who are not trying to hurt their children," he said. "Maybe they want them to go to sleep for an hour so they can go to sleep or go shopping."

In some cases, an adult's warped sense of amusement at seeing a child intoxicated could be the motivation.

"I think somebody might think it's funny," Yin said.

Sedatives were used in more than half the cases Yin studied, often in combination with other drugs. Pain relievers were found in 176 kids; laxatives were used in 67. The average age of the victims was 2, which is consistent with other types of child abuse.

While the number of documented malicious drug-abuse cases was small, Yin says his research is likely just a snapshot of a much larger

Each year, one-hundred-sixty American children are maliciously harmed when forced by parents and other caretakers to take pharmaceuticals.

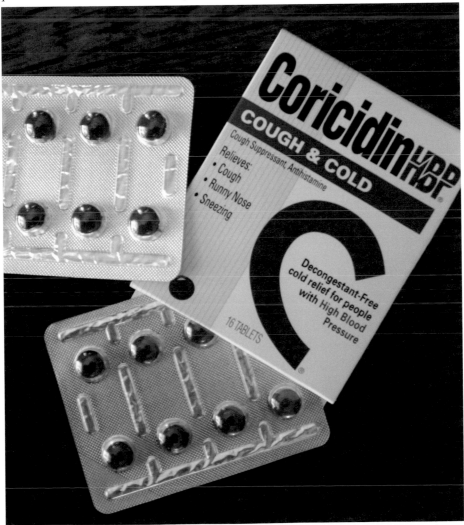

problem. Abuse via malicious drug or alcohol abuse is not captured by current definitions of child maltreatment, which include physical, sexual and emotional abuse and neglect.

When it does occur, not all cases are reported to the nation's poison centers, Yin said.

For instance, the poison center data didn't include the case of William Allen Cunningham, a Georgia man who in 2006 poisoned his 3-year-old son and 18-month-old daughter by feeding them canned soup laced with hot peppers and lighter fluid and later with prescription antidepressants. Cunningham then tried to extort money from the Campbell Soup Co. by claiming the soup was tainted when he bought it.

He was sentenced to 100 years in prison last year, according to news reports.

Links to Physical Abuse

Poisoning likely is occurring in conjunction with other kinds of child abuse, including the nearly 150,000 cases of physical abuse reported each year, Yin said. He'd like to see comprehensive drug screening for children who show up in emergency departments with suspicious injuries.

FAST FACT

The US Centers for Disease Control and Prevention has linked cough and cold medicines to more than fifteen-hundred emergency department visits and three deaths in 2004–2005 among children under two years of age.

Child abuse caused by poisoning is a rare but recognized harm, said Jim Hmurovich, president and chief executive of Prevent Child Abuse America, an advocacy agency. While he had yet to review the new study, Hmurovich said it points to the need for better child abuse prevention efforts.

"I don't think it's right at any time to give unprescribed medicine to a child," he said. "Did the parent do it out of frustration? Did they do it at their wits' end? If that's the case, we need to be even more aggressive in terms of parent education."

Yin said he hopes his study makes people think twice about using drugs to calm children.

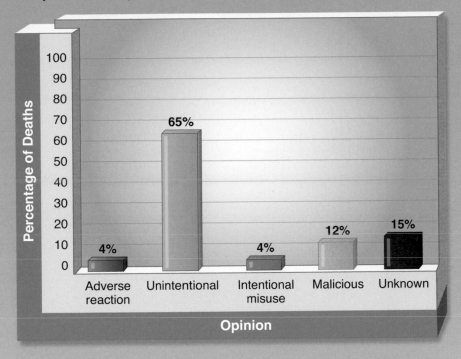

Reasons for Poisoning Deaths of Children Under Five Years Old, 2008

Twenty-six children younger than five died as a result of poisoning in 2008.

Taken from: 2008 Annual Report of the American Association of Poison Control Centers' National Poison Data System.

"For parents, there's a spectrum. I personally know friends who have given children Benadryl on a plane," he said. "But any time you give a child a non-prescribed medication, you run the risk of harming the child."

EVALUATING THE AUTHOR'S ARGUMENTS:

What evidence does JoNel Aleccia use to support her view that child poisonings are a serious problem in the United States? Do you think her argument is persuasive? Why, or why not?

Chapter 2

What Are the Causes of Child Abuse?

Parents addicted to alcohol and/or drugs are more likely to be involved in child abuse.

The Recession Is Linked to an Increase in Child Abuse Cases

"The recession may be provoking an increase in the deadliest form of child abuse."

Liz Szabo

Economic struggles, such as those experienced during a recession, may lead to more cases of violent child abuse directed at the tiniest members of society, maintains Liz Szabo in the following viewpoint. According to Szabo, researchers have found convincing evidence that shaken baby syndrome—a violent form of child abuse typically directed at children less than one year old—increased during the recession that began late in 2007. Szabo says these results are consistent with other studies that link child abuse to poverty and stress. Szabo has been writing about medical topics for *USA Today* since 2004.

AS YOU READ, CONSIDER THE FOLLOWING QUESTIONS:
1. What is the formal name for shaken baby syndrome, according to Szabo?
2. As cited by the author, why were researchers unable to tell whether abuse was linked to job loss?
3. According to Szabo, how can cuts in child protection funding cause numbers of child abuse cases to drop?

Liz Szabo, "Recession Linked to Increase in Shaken Baby Syndrome," *USA Today,* May 3, 2010. From *USA Today,* a division of Gannett Co., Inc. Reprinted with Permission.

T he recession may be provoking an increase in the deadliest form of child abuse, according to a study that finds that the rate of shaken baby syndrome has nearly doubled since the economy collapsed.

Abusive head trauma, as shaken baby syndrome is formally known, often leads to permanent brain damage or paralysis, says co-author Rachel Berger, a child abuse specialist at Children's Hospital of Pittsburgh. She studied 511 cases over five years in four hospitals in Pittsburgh, Cincinnati, Seattle and Columbus, Ohio. Abuse increased in every city; the most dramatic increases were in Seattle and Pittsburgh, she says.

FAST FACT

The concept of shaken baby syndrome was first described in the early 1970s.

Berger acknowledges that a study such as hers can't prove that the recession caused more people to shake their babies. But she believes the link is strong. Berger included only hospitals that employed the same child-protection team throughout the five-year study to ensure that abuse cases were classified the same way before and after the recession began.

And doctors also counted only "unequivocal" cases of child abuse, Berger says.

"We had a high bar, so if anything, we have underestimated the true burden of the problem," says co-author Philip Scribano, medical director of the Center for Child and Family Advocacy at Nationwide Children's Hospital in Columbus.

That makes the findings "quite compelling," says Carole Jenny, a professor of pediatrics at Brown Medical School and Hasbro Children's Hospital in Providence.

Berger's group is the only one "that has studied this in an organized way," Jenny says.

Two-thirds of the children were under age 1, according to the study, presented Saturday at the Pediatric Academic Societies meeting in Vancouver, Canada.

Two-thirds of children were admitted into intensive care, and 16% died, the study says.

Nearly 90% of the children were covered by Medicaid, the government health insurance program for the poor and disabled, both before and after the recession.

Because so many patients were on Medicaid, whose recipients are often unemployed, researchers weren't able to tell whether abuse was linked to job loss, Berger says.

Shaken baby syndrome, or abusive head trauma, often leads to permanent brain damage or paralysis.

Though poor people can be excellent parents, earlier studies have linked child abuse and domestic violence to poverty and stress, says Alice Newton, medical director of the child protection team at Children's Hospital Boston.

Newton says she has seen an increase in especially violent abuse of children, including a baby who was stepped on. Although her hospital typically sees one case of abusive head trauma a month, doctors there have treated six children in the first four months of 2010.

Recessions can contribute to child abuse and death indirectly, Berger says. Cutting funding for child protection can actually cause the number of reported cases to drop—not because fewer children are harmed but because fewer workers are around to file reports, Berger says. States around the country have cut spending for child protection services, she says.

Berger says her study provides a more accurate way to measure child abuse trends.

Because children who survive abusive head trauma are always hospitalized, Berger says, doctors are unlikely to miss any cases—other than victims whose bodies "go straight to the coroner."

EVALUATING THE AUTHOR'S ARGUMENTS:

In this viewpoint Liz Szabo contends that recessions are linked to increases in child abuse. What evidence does she rely on to support her contention? Do you think her viewpoint could use additional evidence? If not, why not? If yes, what type of evidence do you think could be added?

Viewpoint

2

The Recession Is Linked to a Decrease in Child Abuse Cases

David Finkelhor, Lisa Jones, and Anne Shattuck

"Child maltreatment data for 2008 show a generally encouraging situation during the first year of the serious recession that began in late 2007."

In the following viewpoint David Finkelhor, Lisa Jones, and Anne Shattuck maintain that child abuse incidents are down, despite the recession that began in late 2007. Finkelhor, Jones, and Shattuck contend that child abuse data reveal that physical and sexual abuse against children, as well as neglect, were lower in 2008, a year in which there was a full-blown recession. Finkelhor is an American sociologist known for his research into child sexual abuse and related topics. He is the director of Crimes against Children Research Center (CCRC) at the University of New Hampshire. Jones is an assistant professor and Shattuck is a research associate, both at the CCRC.

David Finkelhor, Lisa Jones, and Anne Shattuck, "Updated Trends in Child Maltreatment, 2008," Crimes Against Children Research Center, 2010. Reproduced by permission.

AS YOU READ, CONSIDER THE FOLLOWING QUESTIONS:
1. Between the years 1992 and 2008, which dropped more, physical child abuse or child neglect, according to the authors?
2. As stated in the viewpoint, what study confirms that the trends of declining child abuse rates indicated by the National Child Abuse and Neglect Data System are real and are not statistical or reporting artifacts?
3. According to Finkelhor, Jones, and Shattuck, what is one possible reason that child neglect trends have differed so sharply from those of child sexual and physical abuse?

R ecently released national child maltreatment data for 2008 show a generally encouraging situation during the first year of the serious recession that began in late 2007. Overall substantiated child maltreatment declined 3% from the previous year, including a 6% decline in sexual abuse. Child maltreatment fatalities stayed stable.

National Child Abuse and Neglect Data System

The data . . . are derived from the National Child Abuse and Neglect Data System (NCANDS), which aggregates and publishes statistics from state child protection agencies. The . . . data from NCANDS were released in April 2010 and concern cases of child maltreatment investigated in 2008.

The published NCANDS report shows overall substantiated child maltreatment dropping from 10.6 to 10.3 per 1000 children, a 3% decline in the rate of substantiated child maltreatment from 2007 to 2008. The new rate, equivalent to about 772,000 children, is the lowest level of child maltreatment since the NCANDS system was put into place in 1990.

Disaggregated data from the report show that sexual abuse declined 6% from 2007 to 2008 to a nationally estimated 68,500 substantiated cases. Physical abuse declined 3% to an estimated 119,500 cases. Neglect declined 2% to an estimated 546,600 substantiated cases.

These declines add to an already substantial positive long-term trend, especially for sexual and physical abuse. Sexual abuse has declined 58% from 1992 to 2008, while physical abuse has declined 55%. Neglect has dropped less with only a comparatively small 10% decline since 1992.

It is not possible to directly compare state maltreatment rates because states differ in how statutes define abuse and how abuse is investigated and processed. However, looking at within-state trends, almost all individual states experienced substantial declines in sexual and physical abuse during the period since the early 1990s. Out of the 48 states submitting data to NCANDS, 32 states have seen declines of 50% or more in sexual abuse since 1992. Thirty-one states have seen declines of this size in physical abuse. The data do not show any obvious patterns to the decline by region.

In its data on child maltreatment fatalities, the latest NCANDS shows little change for fatalities for 2008. This is important because the rate rose substantially from 2006 to 2007 (to 2.35 from 2.05 per 100,000), a 15% rise in one year. There was concern that this might be a harbinger of a trend associated with deteriorating economic conditions. But with child maltreatment data, caution needs to be taken in interpreting a single year's fluctuations.

Because NCANDS reports only those cases known to and confirmed by state authorities, questions are always relevant about the extent to which trends reflect changes in reporting practices, investigation standards, and administrative or statistical procedures, not real changes in underlying abuse. These factors can clearly play a role. However, the recently released Fourth National Incidence Study of Child Abuse and Neglect (NIS-4) confirmed that the trends documented in the NCANDS data are not statistical or reporting artifacts. The NIS studies use consistent and standardized definitions of child maltreatment and gather reports directly from professionals in schools, hospitals, day care settings, and other community agencies, avoiding problems created when state agencies

> **FAST FACT**
>
> California, Florida, New York, and Texas are the only states to record having more than one hundred child maltreatment fatalities in 2008, according to the National Child Abuse and Neglect Data System.

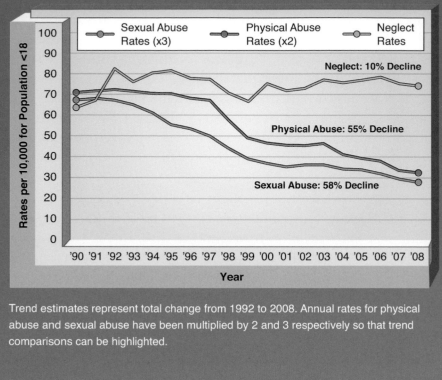

Child Maltreatment Trends, 1990–2008

Trend estimates represent total change from 1992 to 2008. Annual rates for physical abuse and sexual abuse have been multiplied by 2 and 3 respectively so that trend comparisons can be highlighted.

Taken from: David Finkelhor, Lisa Jones, and Anne Shattuck, "Updated Trends in Child Maltreatment, 2008," Crimes Against Children Research Center, 2010.

change their standards, practices or their data systems. The comparison of rates from 1993 to 2005–2006 in NIS-3 and NIS-4 largely tracked the patterns shown in the NCANDS data over the same period, showing a 44% decline in the rate of sexual abuse, a 23% decline in the rate of physical abuse, and no change in the rate of neglect.

In addition, victim self-report surveys conducted across the 1990s and 2000s show declines in sexual offenses and physical assaults against children, further confirming a decline in true underlying incidence.

No Obvious Reason for Declines

There is currently no consensus in the child maltreatment field about why sexual abuse and physical abuse have declined so substantially, although a recent [2006] article and [2008] book [we wrote] suggest some possible factors. The period when sexual and physical abuse started the dramatic downward trend was marked by sustained economic improvement, increases in the numbers of law enforcement and child protection personnel, more aggressive prosecution and incarceration policies, growing public awareness about the problems, and the dissemination of new treatment options for family and mental health problems, including new psychiatric medication. While some have suggested community notification laws as a possible explanatory factor, the passage and implementation of these laws actually occurred well after the sexual abuse decline was underway.

There is no obvious reason why neglect trends have differed so sharply from those of sexual and physical abuse. One possibility is that neglect has not declined because it has not been the subject of the same level of policy attention and public awareness as sexual and physical abuse. Another possibility is that increased education and recent state and professional initiatives about neglect, including the identification of new forms of neglect like drug affected newborns, has masked a decline in other conventional types of neglect.

It is unfortunate that information about the trends in child maltreatment are not better publicized and more widely known. The long-term decline in sexual and physical abuse may have important implications for public policy. These trends deserve more discussion, analysis and research.

EVALUATING THE AUTHORS' ARGUMENTS:

David Finkelhor, Lisa Jones, and Anne Shattuck contend that child abuse rates are lower, despite the recession that began in 2007. After reading this viewpoint and the previous viewpoint by Liz Szabo, what impact do you think recessions have on child abuse? Explain.

Nontraditional Families Are Linked to Child Abuse

Bill Muehlenberg

"If we want to get serious about preventing child abuse, then we should stop peddling the myth that all family structures are equal. They are not."

Children face the greatest risk of child abuse when not living in natural two-parent families, argues Bill Muehlenberg in the following viewpoint. According to Muehlenberg, family structure is very important in determining the risk of a child being abused. There is overwhelming evidence showing that children living in nontraditional family structures such as single-parent households, stepfamilies, and blended families are abused significantly more than children living in traditional families, he says. Muehlenberg believes the best way to prevent child abuse is to increase the number of children living in two-parent biological families. Muehlenberg is an American philosopher and theologian living in Australia. At his blog, *CultureWatch*, he comments on religion, society, and politics.

Bill Muehlenberg, "Child Abuse and Family Structure," CultureWatch.com, July 21, 2009. Reproduced by permission.

1. According to Muehlenberg, the government's response to child abuse is to address what? What does Muehlenberg think the government should concentrate on instead?
2. What is the name of the Australian institute that found that children of single mothers are three times more likely to suffer physical or emotional abuse, according to the author?
3. As cited by the author, a US Department of Justice study found that a cohabitating woman is how many times more likely than a wife to be assaulted?

S ome recent high-profile cases of abused children have once again highlighted the very real problem of child abuse. Anytime a child is abused it is a tragedy. Unfortunately often the response by governments is to address the symptoms instead of concentrating on the causes and dealing with prevention.

Thus there are renewed calls for various types of mandatory reporting, more emphasis on how to identify abuse, and so on. These may have their place, but the real solution would be to reduce the incidence of abuse in the first place. Targeting the causes is crucial here.

And contrary to the thinking of many of our sociologists, bureaucrats, government officials, and ruling elites, family structure really does matter in this regard. That is, not all types of family structure are the same, and some are more likely to result in child abuse than others.

Indeed, the evidence clearly indicates that children are at greatest risk of child abuse when not living in natural two-parent families, but in other family structures, such as blended families, single-parent families, step-families, and so on. The evidence for this has been accumulating for decades now. Here is a small sampling of such data.

Children Are Safest with Their Biological Parents

As one study found, "the risk of abuse and neglect is likely to be exacerbated where substitute individuals fill the roles of biological parents." A study by two Canadian professors of psychology found that when all the variables of class and maternal age are accounted for, "preschoolers in stepparent-natural parent homes . . . are estimated to be *40 times* as likely to become abuse statistics as like-aged children living with two natural parents."

These professors argue that from an evolutionary point of view, no one can or will ever love a child as the genetic parents will. Therefore we can expect less love and commitment shown to a child by a step-parent. They put it this way: "Having a step-parent has turned out to be the most powerful epidemiological risk factor for severe child maltreatment yet discovered." Indeed, they claim that the risk of child abuse and child murder is 100 times greater in a step-parent family than in a genetic family.

In one major study of child abuses cases in which there were children of a previous marriage, it was observed that only step-children were abused and not the natural children. A 1994 study of 52,000 children found that those who are most at risk of being abused are those who are not living with both parents. A Finnish study of nearly 4,000 ninth-grade girls found that "stepfather-daughter incest was about 15 times as common as father-daughter incest."

Or again, it has been found that children in single-parent households are especially vulnerable to abuse, often at the hands of their mother's boyfriends. In Australia, former Human Rights Commissioner Brian Burdekin has reported a 500 to 600 per cent increase in sexual abuse of girls in families where the adult male was not the natural father.

> **FAST FACT**
>
> Out of a total of 1,344 child abuse fatalities in the United States in 2008, 40 were perpetrated by a boyfriend or girlfriend of the parent, according to the US Department of Health and Human Services.

The Australian Institute of Criminology notes that infants under the age of 12 months are the population group at highest risk of being murdered, and the most likely killer of a child is his or her non-biological father—"in other words, the mother's new partner." Furthermore, a study by the Australian Institute of Health and Welfare [AIHW] found that children of single mothers are three times more likely to suffer physical or emotional abuse.

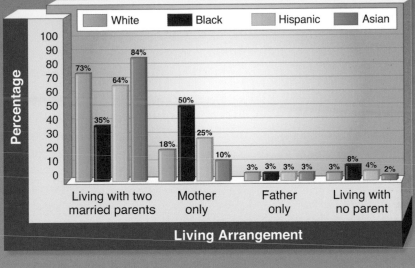

Living Arrangements of Children, by Race and Hispanic Origin, 2009

The information below is based on data from the US Census Bureau's Current Population Survey, 2010, "America's Families and Living Arrangements: 2009." www.census.gov.

Taken from: Child Trends Databank, 2010, www.childrentrendsdatabank.org.

Overwhelming Research

Another study by the AIHW found that more cases of child abuse involved children from single parent families (39%) than families with two natural parents (30%) or other two-parent families (such as families with a step-parent) (21%). Of neglect cases, 47% involved children from female single parent families compared with 26% from families with two natural parents. More recent Australian research has found that the typical child murderer is a young man in a de facto relationship with the victim's mother.

A study of 1998–1999 Victorian [Australian territory] child abuse victims found that 45 per cent lived with single parents. The report, by the Australian Institute of Health and Welfare, found that children who lived in natural two-parent families had a relatively low risk of abuse. And a more recent report from the same Institute entitled *Child Protection Australia 1999–2000* reveals that children are most likely to be neglected or abused in single-parent families. It found that the ACT [Australian Capital Territory] has the highest rate of maltreatment of children from female one-parent families (47 per cent), compared with 29 per cent in two-parent natural families and 18 per cent in step-families or blended families.

And a newer report [2004–2005] from the same body found that "a relatively high proportion of substantiations [of child abuse] involved children living in female-headed one-parent families and in two-parent step or blended families."

And an Australian study of 900 coronial [pertaining to a coroner] inquiries into child deaths found that children were far safer with their biological parents than with step-parents or no biological parents. A study conducted by Deakin University found that children living with a step-parent were 17 to 77 times more likely to die from intentional violence or accident.

The body of Nixzmary Brown is placed into a hearse after her funeral January 18, 2006, in New York City. Brown, seven, was found beaten to death in a Brooklyn apartment. Her mother and stepfather were charged in her death.

A Biological Father Is the Best Protection Against Sexual Abuse

Also, cohabitation is more dangerous for children than is marriage. A U.S. Justice Department study found that a cohabiting woman is 56 times more likely than a wife to be assaulted. And another study found that "cohabitors are more likely to experience violence than are singles or marrieds." It also found that "those males who had cohabited displayed the most accepting views of rape."

American sociologist David Blankenhorn summarises by saying that a "child is sexually safer with her father than with any other man, from a stepfather to her mother's boyfriend to guys in the neighborhood. She is also safer with a father than without one. A child in a fatherless home faces a significantly higher risk of sexual abuse."

There is much more data on this issue which can be cited. But the evidence is overwhelming: if we want to get serious about preventing child abuse, then we should stop peddling the myth that all family structures are equal. They are not.

Sure, there are some children who are abused by their biological parents. But it seems they are in the clear minority. So if we want to turn around high rates of child abuse, then we should do far more to support, nurture and champion the biological two-parent family.

EVALUATING THE AUTHOR'S ARGUMENTS:

Authors use different types of evidence to support their viewpoints. Bill Muehlenberg relies overwhelmingly on statistics to support his contention that children are safest in traditional two-parent families. Examine Muehlenberg's statistics and jot down anything you notice about them. For instance, how many different sources does he use? What are the dates of the studies he cites? And what are the statistics about, i.e., fatalities, sexual abuse, etc.? After examining his statistics, is there anything that makes you change your mind about the strength of his argument? Explain.

Viewpoint 4

Traditional Families Are a Myth

Richard E. Joltes

In the following viewpoint Richard E. Joltes contends that there is no such thing as the "traditional family." According to Joltes, the traditional family exists only in the minds of social conservatives or in 1950s–era TV shows such as *Ozzie and Harriet*. The closest approximation to the traditional family in real life occurred during the two decades right after World War II, when returning soldiers married and raised families, says Joltes. Except for that time period, in most of history, children were raised in single-parent households or Brady Bunch–like conglomerates, or even given away to relatives or charitable organizations, says the author. Joltes is a software developer. He also runs the website Critical Enquiry, which examines the facts behind history and seeks to expose folklores, legends, and myths.

> *"The myth of the 'traditional family' is just that—a myth."*

AS YOU READ, CONSIDER THE FOLLOWING QUESTIONS:
1. According to Joltes, which television show or movie is an accurate representation of the reality of family life in the 1950s?
2. According to Joltes, what were the reasons for the numerous single-parent households prior to the 1950s?
3. What factors does Joltes think are at work in causing many people to believe in the myth of the traditional family?

Richard E. Joltes, "Family Values," Criticalenquiry.org, 2007. Reproduced by permission.

Frequently we hear of conservative groups who long for, and actively seek, what they term a "return to traditional American values." Members of such groups usually are unable to describe the specific time period in which these values are thought to have existed, but can list the alleged "values" nearly verbatim. They consist of the following:

- A two-parent family in which the husband provides financial support while the wife manages home life and childrearing activities. Gender roles are absolute.
- Most (preferably all) members of the family attend some type of Christian church on at least a weekly basis.
- Children are attentive, respectful, bright, and responsible.

Biological Parents Are Most Often Responsible for Child Maltreatment

The data below was collected from US states by the National Child Abuse and Neglect Data System during the period from October 1, 2007, through September 30, 2008. The chart shows the percentage of different parental types who were perpetrators of child maltreatment. Not all states reported. The data revealed that, during this time period, there were 891,809 perpetrators, of which 73.9 percent (658,632 individuals) were parental types of the children.

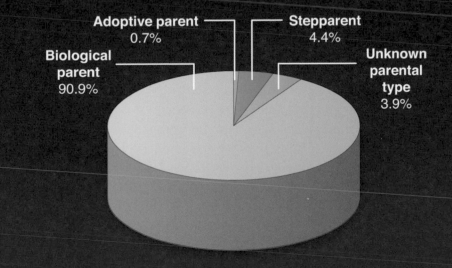

Adoptive parent 0.7%

Stepparent 4.4%

Biological parent 90.9%

Unknown parental type 3.9%

Taken from: US Department of Health and Human Services, *Child Maltreatment 2008*, 2010.

- Families live in the same town, or at least the same vicinity, for generations. Everyone knows their neighbors.
- Divorce is unheard of, and is considered shameful.
- Homosexuality, nonconformist behavior, child abuse, abortion, and domestic abuse do not exist.
- Unmarried couples are extremely rare, and frequently are shunned.
- The number of never-married men ("confirmed bachelors") and women ("spinsters") is extremely low.

This "traditional" mythos recalls the closing lines used by humorist Garrison Keillor at the end of his *Prairie Home Companion* monologues, when he describes his Lake Wobegone community as a place "where all the women are strong, the men are good looking, and the children are above average." It also smacks of an episode of [the TV show] *The Waltons* as well as the movie *Pleasantville*, for reasons that will become apparent.

However, the myth of the "traditional family" is just that—a myth. This "traditional" model has no direct parallel in early US history, and only existed in a limited form during roughly the first two decades of the post World War II era when returning soldiers married and raised families in the Baby Boom. No such two-parent "nuclear" model can be found during earlier periods. While Colonial and later family experiences certainly included mainly two-parent households, they only superficially resembled this wistfully recalled "tradition."

Traditional Families Exist Only in TV Shows

Upon examination, the closest approximation we can find to the family model found so desirable by conservative groups is in 1950s TV shows such as *Father Knows Best, Leave It to Beaver,* and *Ozzie and Harriet* as well as the 1970s *The Waltons.* The first three examples idealized the so-called nuclear family, presenting it as a strongly bonded group managed by a patriarch whose authority was usually absolute. *The Waltons* created the myth of the happy, extended family living together in relative harmony in what was essentially an agrarian paradise. Later, the 1990s movie *Pleasantville* held the "golden age" of the 1950s up to closer inspection, criticizing it as a period when conformism and convention stifled creativity and freedom of expression. This is a more accurate representation of the reality of that decade. . . .

Like many of the family TV shows in the fifties and sixties, Leave It to Beaver *presented an idealized "nuclear family" that was a tightly-bonded group managed by a father whose authority was almost absolute.*

The "Father Knows Best" family is largely the creation of the 1950s. Prior to this period, and after it as well, families were far less cohesive and geographically static.

Fathers Were Frequently Absent

For example, during earlier decades husbands frequently left home to seek work, or embarked on trades requiring extended travel. In the Colonial and Federal periods trappers such as Daniel Boone, whose experiences were later massively embellished by biographers to the point where they only vaguely resembled reality, often spent long periods away from home. During the expansion Westward, men might journey to a newly opened frontier area in order to establish a farm or business, only sending for wife and children once the new venture was operating and stable. Additionally, sailors and others whose business involved travel were away from home for extended periods of time. During these absences, women ran the household and maintained the family's finances. With no means of rapid communication available (letters might take months to reach home, if they arrived at all), the wife and children relied on their own wits as well as assistance—when it was available—from neighbors and community. Periods of separation during this era were often measured in months or years.

This model persisted even as the nation developed. During the Victorian period in both the US and England, husbands often were away from home on military or business journeys. Sailors and businessmen involved in trade frequently traveled for years at a time, with no contact with their families except via occasional letters or money sent home.

People often married at a significantly later age than we now find common; in Victorian England it was not uncommon for lovers to part company at a young age (perhaps as teenagers) to allow a man to travel to India or another far-flung region of the British Empire. Here he would attempt to make his fortune. The couple would only marry much later, once he was financially secure. Often this required upwards of twenty years, which meant some betrothed couples did not actually marry until their mid thirties or even later.

Additionally, high mortality rates due to warfare, illness, and inadequate nutrition resulted in numerous single parent households. Surviving spouses frequently remarried to produce "Brady Bunch"–like family conglomerates. If they did not, they often gave some or all their children to relatives or charitable societies. These children might or might not have contact with their birth parents and siblings later in their lives.

The Women's Role

The role of women prior to the 1950s was also very different. Women experienced a great deal of freedom and economic responsibility as a result of both World War II and the Depression. The war allowed millions of women to work in jobs that otherwise would have remained the realm of men for a much longer period, while the Depression's hardships required both parents to seek employment whenever it was available. Even in the pre-Depression period women experienced a great deal of social and economic freedom. Jobs were relatively plentiful in the 1920s and even earlier, though frequently limited in scope to classic roles such as the secretary, telephone operator, or clerk.

In the pre-Depression period, many women left home for large cities, attended universities, and established their own careers. Clear examples of such independent women include pilots Amelia Earhart and Amy Johnson, as well as suffragette Alice Paul. It should also be noted that the Equal Rights Amendment was passed during this era. In the 1920s, women earned 39 percent of the college degrees in the US, up from 19 percent at the turn of the century. Still earlier, women during the Victorian era were often not directly involved in raising their own children or running the home. Families that could afford them instead opted for governesses and maids who took on these roles.

As noted earlier, these gains were rolled back significantly during the 1950s. The tumult of the Depression, World War II, and perceived Communist threat seems to have produced a desire for "normalcy." This took the form of a quiet, settled, defined family structure. If the outside world was chaotic and threatening, then the home could be made as relaxing and outwardly stress free as possible. Conformism and social stability were enforced as a bulwark against unpredictable, threatening outside forces. Citizens were expected to unite against the perceived outside threat of Soviet/Communist infiltration and attack. A set of "American" values was created and was used as a gauge to measure someone's level of commitment to the nation and the government's programs. Deviation was punished with social ostracism, official suspicion, and (in the case of the [Senator Joseph] McCarthy witch hunt [for Communists]) legal action.

The Role of Children

The perception of the role of children also experienced a significant transformation during the aberrant 1950s. Many scholars argue that the current definition of "childhood" is a modern invention, and only began to emerge among wealthy or privileged families during the 1700s when children began to be dressed or handled differently from adults. Indeed, in agrarian families children were (and are) largely seen as more hands to work the fields and were expected to take on work as soon as they were physically able to do so.

As Capitalism spread in Western Europe and America, more and more children were removed from adult society, treated as adults in development, and exempted from responsibility [for contributing to] the financial success of the family until they reached a specific age. The economic uptick of the 1950s allowed more parents to indulge their children, permitting them to avoid working until they reached the arbitrary age of 16, 18 or 21.

Likewise, the idea that most families stayed in one location is also largely a myth. Later generations often moved further West in order to take advantage of newly opened frontier lands where they might have a better chance of owning large plots of real estate. While some certainly stayed in the same location for generations, genealogical records also show many cases of families living in New England during one period, moving to the mid Atlantic states for a generation or two, then to a territory such as Kansas or the Dakotas, then winding up on the West coast by the early 20th century.

With all the above evidence, why do so many people still believe in the "traditional" family described earlier? No single answer can suffice, but several factors seem to be at work.

Perpetuating the Myth

First and foremost, few people study history beyond the survey courses taught in public school, which often gloss over whole periods in a chapter or two without offering any significant detail. . . .

Another factor in this process is something I've termed "golden age thinking," which describes a nostalgia-filled, often simplistic view of the past based on childhood memories. . . .

In the past, whole societies saw prior eras as "golden ages" in which people were stronger, wiser, more religious, longer lived, or otherwise "better" than in the present.

EVALUATING THE AUTHORS' ARGUMENTS:

What type of evidence does Richard E. Joltes use to support his contention that the concept of a traditional family is a myth? Compare Joltes's viewpoint with the position of Bill Muehlenberg, author of the previous viewpoint, who asserts that the traditional, two-parent, biological family keeps children the safest. With which viewpoint do you agree, and why?

Substance Abuse Causes Parents to Abuse Their Children

Kathryn Wells

"The presence of substance abuse in the home strongly correlates with the recurrence of child maltreatment."

In the following viewpoint a pediatric physician proclaims that children whose parents or caregivers use drugs and alcohol are likely to be abused or neglected. According to Kathryn Wells, the medical director of the Denver Family Crisis Center, children whose parents or caregivers abuse drugs or alcohol live in an unstable environment, where violence, neglect, and other forms of maltreatment are common. Wells says it is important to identify children growing up in such homes in order to protect them and to break the cycle of addiction, since children whose parents abuse substances face a high risk of being substance abusers themselves.

AS YOU READ, CONSIDER THE FOLLOWING QUESTIONS:
1. According to Wells, a survey of state child protection service agencies indicates that substance abuse was one of the two leading problems exhibited by families reported for child maltreatment. What was the other leading problem identified?

2. According to Wells, a study by Jeanne Reid and her colleagues from the National Center on Addiction and Substance Abuse indicates that substance abuse shows a significant association with what severe outcome of child abuse?
3. What does Wells say are some of the outcomes for children who grow up in homes where substance abuse is an issue?

Epidemiology

Research has confirmed a strong connection between substance abuse and child maltreatment.[2,3] In one study that controlled for many variables, children whose parents were abusing substances were found to be 2.7 times more likely to be abused and 4.2 times more likely to be neglected than other children whose parents were not substance abusers.[3-5] In a 1998 survey of the 50 state child protection service agencies, the National Committee to Prevent Child Abuse (now Prevent Child Abuse America) reported that 85% of the states indicated that substance abuse was one of the two leading problems exhibited by families reported for child maltreatment[6] with poverty being the other most frequently reported issue. Review of juvenile court data in one study showed that, in 43% of cases of serious child abuse or neglect, at least one parent had a documented problem with either alcohol or drugs and instances of substance abuse allegedly took place in 50%

FAST FACT

According to the US Substance Abuse and Mental Health Services Administration, more than 6 million children, or about 9 percent of all children in the United States, live with at least one parent who abuses or is dependent on alcohol or an illicit drug.

of the cases.[7] This study also showed that parents with documented substance abuse, in comparison with parents with no documented substance abuse, were more likely to have been previously charged with child maltreatment and were also more likely to be rated as high risk to their children, more likely to reject court-ordered services, and were more likely to have their children permanently removed.

Parental substance abuse has been linked to the most serious outcomes of all cases of child maltreatment, including fatalities. Data by Reid and colleagues[8] indicate that substance abuse by caregivers is associated with as many as two thirds of all cases of child maltreatment fatalities.[8] In this study, 51% of these deaths involved physical abuse while 44% involved neglect and 5% involved multiple forms of child maltreatment.

The combined stresses of substance abuse and routine care of infants and children can create an environment of physical abuse and neglect.

Children Living with Substance-Abusing Parents, 2001

The data below shows the estimated numbers of children aged seventeen or younger living with one or more substance-abusing parents in 2003.

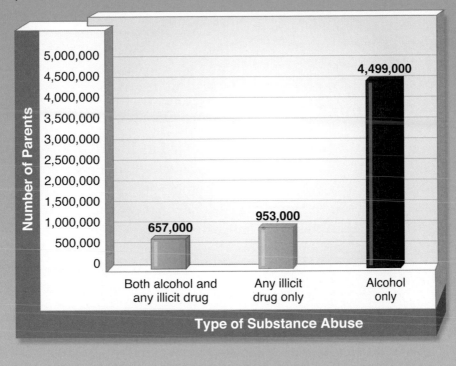

Taken from: National Household Survey on Drug Abuse, "Children Living with Substance-Abusing or Substance-Dependent Parents," Office of Applied Studies, Substance Abuse and Mental Health Services Administration, June 2, 2003.

Substance Abuse As Risk for Child Maltreatment

The combined stresses of substance abuse and the demands for the routine care of infants and children can create a volatile or otherwise vulnerable environment in which neglect or physical abuse can occur. Parents or caregivers who are acutely intoxicated or withdrawing from drugs or alcohol will not respond appropriately to the cues an infant or child gives for both physical and social interactive nurturing. A parent or caregiver who abuses substances has impaired judgment and priorities and is unable to provide the consistent care, supervision, and guidance that children need. Additionally, these homes are often plagued with other problems, including physical or mental illness; poor parenting skills; domestic violence; involvement of caregivers with drugs, alcohol, and criminal activity; and lack of such resources as money, time, energy, and emotional support for the children. Finally, many drugs of abuse make adult caregivers violent, paranoid, and angry, creating a situation where the caregiver is more prone to injure or neglect their children.[9] For all these reasons, substance abuse is clearly a critical factor in child welfare.[10] Along with previous referrals to child protective services, history of domestic violence, history of caregiver child abuse and neglect as a child, and caregiver impairments, the presence of substance abuse in the home strongly correlates with the recurrence of child maltreatment.[11]

To break the cycles of addiction and child maltreatment, children at risk in environments where substance abuse takes place must be identified. Children who grow up in homes where substance abuse is an issue have poorer outcomes (behaviorally, psychologically, socially, and physically) than children whose parents or caregivers do not abuse substances. Without intervention, these children are at increased risk of substance abuse themselves. Children who were abused during their childhood have a greater risk of substance abuse later in life, highlighting the importance of breaking this cycle of addiction.[12]

Children in homes where alcohol is being abused or drugs are being used are exposed to many risks ranging from prenatal exposure and the effects it may have on the fetus to potential exposure to the drugs themselves and exposure to a violent and chaotic environment. Affected families must be identified so that the children can be properly evaluated and an ongoing safety plan can be established.

EVALUATING THE AUTHOR'S ARGUMENTS:

How strongly do you think Kathryn Wells made her point that substance abuse is linked to child abuse? What impact do you think her profession has on the credibility of her position? Explain.

References

2. Child Welfare League of America & North American Commission on Chemical Dependency and Child Welfare. Children at the front; a different view of the war on alcohol and drugs. Washington, DC: Child Welfare League of America; 1992.

3. White WL, Illinois Department of Children and Family Services, Illinois Department of Alcoholism and Substance Abuse. SAFE 95: a status report on Project Safe, an innovative project designed to break the cycle of maternal substance abuse and child neglect/abuse. Springfield (IL): Illinois Department of Children and Family Services; 1995.

4. Kelleher K, Chaffin M, Hollenberg J, et al. Alcohol and drug disorders among physically abusive and neglectful parents in a community-based sample. Am J Public Health 1994;84:1586–90.

5. Health and Human Services, Public Health Service, Substance Abuse and Mental Health Services Administration & Office of Applied Studies. National household survey on drug abuse: main findings, 1996. Rockville (MD): Substance Abuse and Mental Health Services Administration, Office of Applied Studies; 1998.

6. Wang CT, Harding K. Current trends in child abuse reporting and fatalities: the results of the 1998 annual fifty state survey. Chicago: National Committee to Prevent Child Abuse; 1999.

7. Murphy JM, Jellinew M, Quinn D, et al. Substance abuse and serious child maltreatment: prevalence, risk, and outcome in a court sample. Child Abuse Negl 1991;15:197–211.

8. Reid J, Macchetto P, Foster S. No safe haven: children of substance-abusing parents. New York: National Center on Addiction and Substance Abuse at Columbia University; 1999.

9. Bays J. Substance abuse and child abuse—impact of addiction on the child. Pediatr Clin North Am 1990;37:881–904.

10. U.S. Department of Health and Human Services. Blending perspectives and building common ground: a report to congress on substance abuse and child protection. Washington DC: US Government Printing Office; 1999.

11. English DJ, Marshall DB, Brummel S, et al. Characteristics of repeated referrals to child protective services in Washington State. Child Maltreat 1999; 4(4):297–307.

12. Bennett EM, Kemper KJ. Is abuse during childhood a risk factor for developing substance abuse problems as an adult? J Dev Behav Pediatr 1994;15:426–9.

Viewpoint
6

Homosexuality Causes Child Sexual Abuse

Bob Ellis

"The love between men and boys is at the foundation of homosexuality."

In the following viewpoint Bob Ellis contends that a strong link exists between homosexuality and the sexual abuse of young boys. Ellis cites several studies indicating that homosexuals molest young boys significantly more often than heterosexuals molest young girls. According to Ellis, these studies and other evidence suggest that homosexuality is the cause of a large proportion of child sexual abuse. He thinks a tragic cycle exists in which young boys who are sexually molested grow up to become homosexuals and potential child molesters themselves. Ellis runs the online news website *Dakota Voice,* which provides a conservative Christian commentary on issues in the news.

AS YOU READ, CONSIDER THE FOLLOWING QUESTIONS:

1. Who is the author of the report highlighted by *LifeSiteNews* and the source of Ellis's "interesting findings"?
2. According to Ellis, in what year did Alfred Kinsey do his research on homosexuality?
3. According to Ellis, a study discussed in an article published by an English organization provides an indication of why there is a connection between homosexuality and child molestation. What did the study find?

Bob Ellis, "Report: Homosexuality Connected to Sex Abuse Epidemic," *Dakota Voice,* April 20, 2010. Reproduced by permission.

*L*ifeSiteNews [an online news site] highlights a very interesting report by Brian Clowes, director of Human Life International Research on the question of homosexuality and pedophilia.

The Question of Homosexuality and Pedophilia

While this question goes back a few decades with regard to the highly publicized cases of child molestation at the hands of a number of Catholic priests, the question again came to prominence about a year ago [in 2009] when it came to light that Associate Director of Duke University's Center for Health Policy Frank Lombard was molesting a 5-year-old boy he adopted. Lombard was caught by undercover police while online under the screen name "Perv Dad for Fun" inviting these undercover officers to travel to North Carolina to rape the boy as he had already done.

FAST FACT

According to the fourth National Incidence Study of Child Abuse and Neglect, 87 percent of sexually abused children were abused by a male, compared with only 11 percent by a female.

At that time, I cited Judith Reisman, president of the Institute for Media Education, who stated Department of Justice data shows that 64% of forcible sodomy victims are boys under 12, and that Dr. Gene Abel, director of the Behavioral Medicine Institute in Atlanta, performed a study which found that homosexuals sexually molest young boys with an incidence five times greater than the molestation rate of girls; 150 boys are molested by one male homosexual versus 19.8 girls by heterosexual molesters.

Troubling Findings

Returning now to the report by Clowes, he examined research going back more than 60 years with some interesting findings:

- Alfred Kinsey, himself a homosexual and no conservative religious "homophobe" by anyone's imagination, did research in 1948 in which he reported 37% of all male homosexuals admitted having sex with children under 17.

- A recent study in the *Archives of Sexual Behavior* found that while less than 3% of men attracted to adults are homosexual, 25–40% of men attracted to children preferred boys, meaning a homosexual attraction is 6–20 times higher among pedophiles.
- Another study in that same journal found that only 39 of 48 homosexual men examined in a study preferred the two youngest male age categories: 15- and 20-year-olds.
- Yet another study in the *Archives of Sexual Behavior* again found less than 3% homosexuality in men attracted to adults, but homosexuality among pedophiles as high as 30–40%.
- A study in the *Journal of Sex Research* found the proportion of sex offenders against male children much higher than the molestation rate against female children by heterosexual men.
- A study in the *Archives of Sexual Behavior* found 86% of sex offenders against males identified themselves as homosexual or bisexual.
- Department of Health and Human Services statistics show that among priests who molest children, 6 out of 7 molest boys.
- [In] an editorial in the *San Francisco Sentinel*, a member of the National Lesbian & Gay Journalist's Association stated that "the love between men and boys is at the foundation of homosexuality. For the gay community to imply that boy-love is not homosexual love is ridiculous."
- Larry Kramer, founder of the homosexual group AIDS Coalition to Unleash Power (ACT-UP), said that "I submit that often, very often, the child desires the activity, and perhaps even solicits it, either because of a natural curiosity, or because he or she is homosexual and innately knows it."
- Pat Califia, lesbian author and activist, wrote in the "mainstream" homosexual publication *The Advocate*, "Instead of condemning pedophiles for their involvement with lesbian and gay youth, we should be supporting them."
- The American Psychiatric Association (APA) recently sponsored a symposium in which participants discussed the removal of pedophilia from an upcoming edition of the group's psychiatric manual of mental disorders.
- In 1988, a leading American psychological journal, *Behavior Today*, claimed that "Pedophilia may be a sexual orientation rather than a sexual deviation. This raises the question as to whether pedophiles may have rights."

This vase depicts the classical representation of Greek homosexual love, a relationship between a man and a young boy. The author contends that homosexuality and child sexual molestation are connected.

These are very troubling findings—including these statements that excuse, condone and legitimize child molestation. But why such a substantial connection between homosexuality and child molestation?

The Cycle of Sexual Molestation

The answers are probably complicated, but there are some strong indicators. AidsMan [an AIDS information organization] in England published an article last year [2009] concerning the link between childhood sexual abuse and risky sexual behavior. Of the 4,244 homosexual men in the study, 40% of them reported childhood sexual abuse. When nearly half of the subjects report that they have been molested as children, a strong link is indicated.

How do we end such a heart-breaking cycle of sexual molestation? Probably no easy answer exists, but one thing is certain: pretending these links don't exist, and pretending that aberrant sexual behavior is normal and natural won't move us any closer to a solution.

EVALUATING THE AUTHOR'S ARGUMENTS:

In this viewpoint Bob Ellis contends that because more boys are sexually molested by homosexual men than girls are molested by heterosexual men, it must mean that homosexuality and child sexual molestation are connected. What do you think about the logic of Ellis's contention? Explain.

Homosexuality Does Not Cause Child Sexual Abuse

Joe Kort

"The research to date all points to there being no significant relationship between a homosexual lifestyle and child molestation."

It is wrong to link pedophilia and homosexuality, argues Joe Kort in the following viewpoint, because pedophiles generally do not care about the gender of their victims. Kort says that pedophiles are neither gay nor straight, since they do not desire adults of either sex. Pedophiles are not perpetrating a homosexual act against children, he says. Instead, they are using sex as a tool for violence and exploitation and will molest children who are accessible to them, regardless of their gender. Kort thinks prejudice is the most likely reason that people blame homosexuals for child molestation. Kort is an author and nationally recognized psychotherapist specializing in gay and lesbian issues.

Joe Kort, From "Gay's Anatomy: Homosexuality and Pedophilia: The False Link," *Psychology Today Blogs,* September 15, 2008. Reproduced by permission.

1. How does Gregory Herek define pedophilia, as cited in the viewpoint?
2. According to Kort, pedophiles use sex as a weapon. This is similar to what other crime that feminists have been arguing for years is not a sex act?
3. As stated by Kort, what other groups of people does Herek say were widely accused of violent acts in order to justify discrimination?

Q: I've heard therapists say that a male adult who sexually abuses a boy isn't necessarily "homosexual." This seems confusing: If he isn't homosexual, then why would he sexually molest boys, instead of girls?

This is a very good question, and there are several ways to respond to it. First, we need to clarify our definitions. When discussing sexual abuse and molestation of children, there's often conflict over terminology. One frequently quoted researcher on the topic of homosexuality and child molestation, Gregory Herek, a research psychologist at the University of California, defines pedophilia as "a psychosexual disorder characterized by a preference for prepubescent children as sexual partners, which may or may not be acted upon." He defines child sexual abuse as "actual sexual contact between an adult and someone who has not reached the legal age of consent." Not all pedophiles actually molest children, he points out. A pedophile may be attracted to children, but never actually engage in sexual contact with them. Quite often, pedophiles never develop a sexual orientation toward other adults.

Herek points out that child molestation and child sexual abuse refer to "actions," without implying any "particular psychological makeup or motive on the part of the perpetrator." In other words, not all incidents of child sexual abuse are perpetrated by pedophiles. Pedophilia can be viewed as a kind of sexual fetish, wherein the person requires the mental image of a child—not necessarily a flesh-and-blood child—to achieve sexual gratification. Rarely does a pedophile experience sexual desire for adults of either gender. They usually don't identify as homosexual—the majority identify as heterosexual, even those who abuse children of the same gender. They are sexually aroused by youth, not by gender. In contrast, child molesters often exert power and control over children in an effort to dominate them. They do experience sexual desire for adults, but molest children episodically, for reasons apart from sexual desire, much as rapists enjoy power, violence and controlling their humiliated victims. Indeed, research supports that a child molester isn't any more likely to be homosexual than heterosexual.

In fact, some research shows that for pedophiles, the gender of the child is immaterial. Accessibility is more the factor in who a pedophile abuses. This may explain the high incidence of children molested in church communities and fraternal organizations, where the pedophile may more easily have access to children. In these situations, an adult male is trusted by those around him, including children and their families. Males are often given access to boys to mentor, teach, coach and advise. Therefore, a male pedophile may have easier access to a male

The author contends that "a pedophile abusing a child of the same sex is not perpetrating a homosexual act, but an act of violence and exploitation using sexuality." Thus, he argues, people should not equate pedophilia with homosexuality.

child. In trying to make sense of an adult male's sexually abusing a male child, many of us mislabel it as an act of homosexuality, which it isn't.

Feminists have argued for years that rape is not a sex act—it is an act of violence using sex as a weapon. In the same way, a pedophile abusing a child of the same sex is not perpetrating a homosexual act, but an act of violence and exploitation using sexuality. There is a world of difference between these two things, but it requires a subtle understanding of the inner motivation of the abuser.

To call child molestation of a boy by a man "homosexual" or of a girl by a man "heterosexual" is to misunderstand pedophilia. No true pedophile is attracted to adults, so neither homosexuality nor heterosexuality applies. Accordingly, Herek suggests calling men's sexual abuse of boys "male-male molestation" and men's abuse of girls, "male-female molestation."

Interestingly, Anna C. Salter writes, in "Predators, Pedophiles, Rapists and other Sex Offenders", that when a man molests little girls, we call him a "pedophile" and not a "heterosexual." Of course, when a man molests little boys, people say outright, or mutter under their breath, "homosexual." Herek writes that because of our society's aversion to male homosexuality, and the attempts made by some to represent gay men as a danger to "family values," many in our society immediately think of male-male molestation as homosexuality. He compares this with the time when African Americans were often falsely accused of raping white women, and when medieval Jews were accused of murdering Christian babies in ritual sacrifices. Both are examples of how mainstream society eagerly jumped to conclusions that justified discrimination and violence against these minorities. Today, gays face the same kind of prejudice. Most recently, we've seen gay men unfairly turned out of the Boy Scouts of America on the basis of this myth that gay men are likely to be child molesters. Keeping gays out of scouting won't protect boys from pedophiles.

Girls Are Sexually Abused More Often than Boys Are

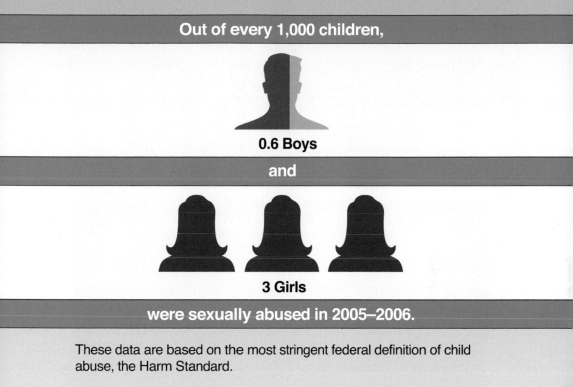

Out of every 1,000 children,

0.6 Boys

and

3 Girls

were sexually abused in 2005–2006.

These data are based on the most stringent federal definition of child abuse, the Harm Standard.

Taken from: Fourth National Incidence Study of Child Abuse and Neglect (NIS-4), Report to Congress, US Department of Health and Human Services, 2010.

In reality, abuse of boys by gay pedophiles is rare, and the abuse of girls by lesbians is rarer still. Nicholas Groth is a noted authority on this topic. In a 1982 study by Groth, he asks, "Are homosexual adults in general sexually attracted to children, and are pre-adolescent children at greater risk of molestation from homosexual adults than from heterosexual adults? There is no reason to believe so. The research to date all points to there being no significant relationship between a homosexual lifestyle and child molestation. There appears to be practically no reportage of sexual molestation of girls by lesbian adults, and the adult male who sexually molests young boys is not likely to be homosexual." Herek writes, similarly, that abuse of boys by gay men is rare; and that the abuse of girls by lesbians is rarer still.

The topic of female-female molestation continues to be largely ignored. There are few books on female sex offenders, particularly about mothers sexually abusing their daughters. I can find only one book on mothers who sexually abuse their sons by Hani Miletski, M.S.W., entitled, "Mother-Son Incest: The Unthinkable Taboo." Unthinkable is an appropriate word—so much so that there is nothing else in the literature on this topic, even though female pedophiles and female child molesters certainly exist.

We know so much more than we did historically and yet have a long way to go. We can understand child sexual abuse further when people's bias and prejudice are removed and the evidence is empirical and scientific.

EVALUATING THE AUTHORS' ARGUMENTS:

In this viewpoint Joe Kort argues that child molestation, when perpetrated by a pedophile, has nothing to do with gender and that it is therefore wrong to link homosexuality and child molestation. What do you think about the logic of Kort's contention? Which viewpoint, Kort's or the previous selection by Bob Ellis, do you think is more logical? Which do you think has more evidence to support it? With which position do you agree, and why?

Chapter 3

What Is the Best Way to Prevent Child Abuse?

Many child advocacy groups and centers for the prevention of child abuse have opened across the country, such as this one in Niceville, Florida.

Viewpoint

1

Child Abuse Prevention Is a Public Health Concern

Francie Zimmerman and James A. Mercy

"Some of our nation's most serious health concerns can be linked to trauma from abuse and neglect early in life."

In the following viewpoint Francie Zimmerman and James A. Mercy contend that child abuse prevention, which currently focuses on individual families, should use a public health approach and focus on preventing child abuse in the entire community. In contrast with primary care physicians, who concern themselves with the health of their individual patients, public health practitioners focus on disease prevention and other efforts that try to make entire communities healthier. Zimmerman and Mercy think this approach to child abuse prevention can be successful. By preventing child abuse at the community level, before individual instances occur, the health of communities and society as a whole will be increased, say the authors.

Zimmerman is program director of the Doris Duke Charitable Foundation's Child Abuse Prevention Program, and Mercy is a special adviser in the Division of Violence

Francie Zimmerman and James A. Mercy, "A Better Start: Child Maltreatment Prevention as a Public Health Priority," Zero to Three, May 2010. Reproduced by permission.

Prevention at the US Centers for Disease Control and Prevention's National Center for Injury Prevention and Control. Their article was published by the national nonprofit organization called Zero to Three, which seeks to improve the lives of infants and toddlers.

AS YOU READ, CONSIDER THE FOLLOWING QUESTIONS:
1. What analogy from the environmental field do Zimmerman and Mercy use to describe the public health approach to addressing child abuse?
2. According to the authors, how many public health employees, on average, are employed by each state?
3. According to Zimmerman and Mercy, what is the umbrella name for an array of strategies that integrates child abuse prevention into early education and child care programs?

I magine a community where all of the adults who interact with children—parents, family members, child care providers, teachers, doctors, nurses, clergy, and neighbors—actively engage in preventing child maltreatment *before* an incident of abuse or neglect occurs. Imagine a community where there is a wide continuum of prevention activities that extends well beyond providing direct services to individual families; a continuum that includes public education efforts to change social norms and behavior, neighborhood activities that engage parents, and public policies and institutions that support families. This type of broad-based, communitywide approach is often the purview of public health systems, because public health strategies, by definition, strive to promote the health and well-being of populations as a whole.

A Public Health Approach

A public health approach to child maltreatment would address the range of conditions that place children at risk for abuse or neglect, not just at the individual and family levels but also at the community and societal levels. To use an analogy from the environmental field, a public health approach expands the focus from individual "endangered animals" to encompass the broader "habitat and

Shown here is a new children's advocacy center located in Massachusetts. At centers like this one, policies and programs are implemented that educate families about child abuse.

environmental factors" that place species at risk. Historically, most child abuse prevention programs focused on individual and family dynamics, not communitywide or population-based strategies. That is changing. A growing number of practitioners and policymakers are implementing prevention efforts outside of the child welfare system in community settings that see large numbers of families with young children.

Although state and local departments of health do utilize comprehensive public health strategies, they typically do *not* address the specific problem of child maltreatment. This is a critical missed opportunity because, in addition to the immediate harm to children, there is a growing body of evidence that early traumatic experiences are associated with health problems throughout the lifespan. In fact, research shows an association between child maltreatment and a broad range of problems including substance abuse, intimate partner violence, teenage pregnancy, anxiety, depression, suicide, diabetes, ischemic heart disease, sexually transmitted diseases, smoking, and obesity. Some of our nation's most serious health concerns can be linked to trauma from abuse and neglect early in life. Preventing maltreatment can be a powerful lever to move the population toward greater health and well-being.

The Magnitude of Abuse and Neglect

Child maltreatment—which includes physical, sexual, and emotional abuse and neglect—is a problem of significant scope. In 2007, public child protective services agencies received reports of alleged maltreatment involving 5.8 million children. That is more than six times the number of children enrolled in all Head Start programs for the same year. Sixty-two percent of reports to child protective services, involving 3.5 million children, were screened for further investigation or assessment (a rate of 47 children reported per 1,000 children in the general population); 794,000 were determined to be victims of abuse or neglect. In 86% of these cases, parents or other relatives were responsible for the maltreatment. Neglect was the problem in 60% of the cases. Young children, under 7 years old, constitute the majority of child abuse/neglect cases (55.7%) and suffer the greatest harm. Infants less than 1 year old have the highest rates of child victimization at 22 victims per 1,000 children.

The number of children officially reported to child protection systems substantially undercounts the total population of children who experience abuse or neglect. Conducted in 2008, the National Survey of Children's Exposure to Violence (NatSCEV) was the first national study to examine children's exposure to violence in homes, schools, and communities across all age groups. In terms of maltreatment, NatSCEV found that more than 1 in 10 children surveyed (10.2%) suffered some form of maltreatment during the past year and nearly 1 in 5 (18.6%) did so during their lifetimes. In contrast to the reports to public child welfare agencies noted earlier, rates of exposure to maltreatment from NatSCEV rose as children grew older. This is perhaps due to greater underreporting of maltreatment perpetrated against older children to public welfare agencies.

Consequences of Abuse and Neglect

For decades, the negative impact of abuse and neglect on children has been documented to include injuries, disabilities, and other physical

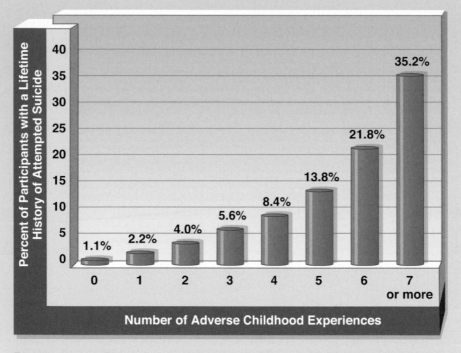

The Number of Adverse Childhood Experiences and Lifetime History of Attempted Suicide

Seventeen thousand US adults were asked if they had experienced as children the following types of abuse:

* Emotional abuse
* Physical abuse
* Sexual abuse
* Emotional neglect
* Physical neglect

* Violence towards mother
* Household substance abuse
* Household mental illness
* Incarcerated household member
* Divorce or separation

Percent of Participants with a Lifetime History of Attempted Suicide

40
35
30
25
20
15
10
5
0

1.1%   2.2%   4.0%   5.6%   8.4%   13.8%   21.8%   35.2%

0   1   2   3   4   5   6   7 or more

Number of Adverse Childhood Experiences

Taken from: Jennifer S. Middlebrooks and Natalie C. Audage, *The Effects of Childhood Stress on Health Across the Lifespan*, Centers for Disease Control and Prevention, National Center for Injury Prevention and Control, 2008.

health issues; low academic achievement; and emotional problems. In recent years, newer brain imaging techniques have enabled scientists to document the effects of abuse and neglect on the developing brain and, hence, a broader range of health and social consequences of abuse and neglect. These images show that maltreatment early in life actually damages the brain's physical structure by impairing cell growth, interfering with the formation of health circuitry, and altering the neural structure and function of the brain itself.

Jack Shonkoff, director of Harvard University's Center on the Developing Child, explains that "there is extensive evidence that adversity can get 'under the skin' and undermine health and development. Persistent stress produces excessive elevation in heart rate, blood pressure, and stress hormones which can impair brain architecture, immune status, metabolic systems, and cardiovascular function."

Thus, early life experiences are built into our bodies. Abuse, neglect, and other traumatic events can take a serious toll, contributing to health problems over a lifetime. The Adverse Childhood Experiences Study [ACE] provides powerful evidence of this. The [ACE] is an ongoing study of over 17,000 primarily middle-class adults who are enrolled in the Kaiser Permanente health care system and who provided retrospective information about their childhoods. This study found that individuals who experienced five or more adversities (e.g., abuse, neglect, family dysfunction) were at fivefold greater risk for depression. Perhaps, the impact of early adversity on emotional well-being is not surprising, but the [ACE] also found that an individual who had seven adverse experiences has a 10-fold greater likelihood of having heart disease. Recent findings from the ongoing [ACE] indicate that early trauma is associated with shorter life expectancy. The researchers found that people with six or more adverse childhood experiences died nearly 20 years earlier on average than those without such experiences. Those who suffered substantial childhood trauma have double the risk for early death, compared with adults who had not endured adverse childhood experiences.

FAST FACT

It is estimated that approximately one-third of abused and neglected children will eventually victimize their own children, according to Prevent Child Abuse New York.

The Contribution to Health Disparities

Exposure to child maltreatment is not randomly distributed within populations. The likelihood of a child experiencing maltreatment is associated with her or his social and economic environment. Children from households with lower income and parental education and who live in communities with greater concentrations of disadvantage, housing stress, low social capital, and lack of social support are more likely to be exposed to child maltreatment. These exposures exacerbate and sustain socioeconomic, racial, and ethnic health disparities across generations by compromising a child's health, cognitive abilities, and social skills over the course of his or her life. Therefore, although not currently recognized as such, the prevention of maltreatment may be critically important to reducing social and economic disparities in health.

A Role for Public Health
Public health infrastructure exists in every state, with an average of about 2,000 state employees in the workforce and state and federal funding of approximately $2.89 billion combined per state. However, championing a public health approach does not mean transferring responsibility from one public agency to another. Rather, a successful public health strategy would weave together programs, policies, and people. Such an approach would entail engaging a host of partners from other service systems (e.g., early education, schools, police, health care, parent education, and family support), as well as community-based resources (e.g., faith-based organizations, neighborhood leaders, libraries, recreation centers). Such a strategy would also entail educating the public through media and other outreach efforts. Cumulatively, public health strategies would influence individual behavior and build public will to support policy changes that promote healthy child development.

Think of the shift that has occurred, for example, with cigarette smoking. Antismoking efforts have moved well beyond educational programs urging individuals to quit, to policies that limit exposure to secondhand smoke and increase taxes on cigarettes—all aimed at reducing health problems caused by smoking. In combination, these elements have changed how society views cigarettes and have reduced U.S. smoking rates over time.

Child abuse and neglect prevention efforts have already moved significantly into public health terrain. Over the past decade, many prevention efforts have evolved from a narrow focus on individual victims involved in the child welfare system to a wider repertoire of prevention strategies that reach more families and are based in normal, nonstigmatizing places. There is strong momentum; new partnerships and programs show great promise for reducing risk and enhancing protective factors for children. Child abuse prevention is moving from a reactive to a proactive stance. Ultimately, through coordination between our child protective service and public health systems, an optimal balance can be achieved between these reactive and proactive elements of child maltreatment prevention. . . .

Strengthening Families is the umbrella name for an array of strategies—including staff training, program enhancements, quality improvement efforts and policy changes—that integrate prevention into early education and child care programs. Dozens of states and localities are engaged in some type of Strengthening Families activity which is spearheaded by the Center for the Study of Social Policy and promoted by other national organizations such as ZERO TO THREE Children's Trust and Prevention Funds, and the United Way. There is evidence that enriched early education programs can achieve prevention goals. The Chicago Longitudinal Study found that children who participated in the Child Parent Centers (which provided early education and family support services) had a 52% lower rate of substantiated maltreatment by age 17 than children in the comparison group who attended regular kindergarten.

EVALUATING THE AUTHORS' ARGUMENTS:

What main ideas do Francie Zimmerman and James A. Mercy use to support their contention that child abuse prevention efforts should be based on a public health approach? In your opinion, is the public health approach a good way to prevent child abuse? Why or why not?

In-Home Parent Education Programs Can Help Prevent Child Abuse

"There is a growing body of evidence that some home visitation programs can be a successful child maltreatment prevention strategy."

Maiso Bryant

In the following viewpoint Maiso Bryant discusses the background and reasons for giving government support to home-visitation programs. Typical home visitation programs provide information on parenting, child development, and community resources. Home visitors work to reduce stress and improve the ability of the parent to care for the child or children. Although not all home visitation programs produce positive results, those that target the most at-risk families, that remain in effect in the home for longer than two years, or that employ trained nurses as the home visitors are among those that do show positive outcomes, according to Bryant.

Maiso Bryant, "Program Announcement: Background Supporting Evidence-Based Home Visitation Programs to Prevent Child Maltreatment," Department of Health and Human Services, Administration for Children and Families, Administration on Children, Youth and Families, Children's Bureau, May 16, 2008. www.supportingebhv.org.

At the time of writing, Bryant was acting commissioner for administration on children, youth and families—a part of the Administration for Children and Families (ACF), under the US Department of Health and Human Services.

AS YOU READ, CONSIDER THE FOLLOWING QUESTIONS:
1. What is the most important means available to address maltreatment of children, according to the author.
2. What positive short-term and intermediate outcomes does Bryant say the typical home visitation program hopes to produce?
3. What families have the highest risk factors for child maltreatment, according to the author?

G iven the limited funding available to support human services programs and the push towards more accountability for outcomes, policymakers have become much more selective and insistent that funding support evidence-based programs that have demonstrated positive results. Over the last several years there has been sustained growth in the focus on identifying and using evidence-based programs and practices for a variety of disciplines such as health, mental health, substance abuse, education, juvenile justice, and child welfare programs. Prevention is the most important means available to address child maltreatment. There is a growing body of evidence that some home visitation programs can be a successful child maltreatment prevention strategy.

Although there are a range of different models, the typical home visitation program uses home visiting as the primary strategy for the delivery of services to families. These services can include providing information about parenting and child development, linking families to other community services and resources and providing social support. Through the efforts of the home visitor to engage and establish a strong relationship with the family, it is hoped that the program will produce short-term and intermediate positive outcomes such as changes in parent knowledge and behavior, decreased stress, better family functioning, and access to needed services. The long-term outcomes generally include better child health outcomes, better social and emotional support for the families, increased capacity of a parent to care for the child, and decreased abuse or neglect.

There is a sizable body of research, using both experimental and quasi-experimental study designs, that has evaluated the impact of a few nationally recognized home visitation programs. In addition, there have been a number of research reviews, meta-analyses, syntheses of findings and commentaries regarding the effectiveness of various home visitation programs. A systematic review of the research on early childhood home visitation programs found that such approaches

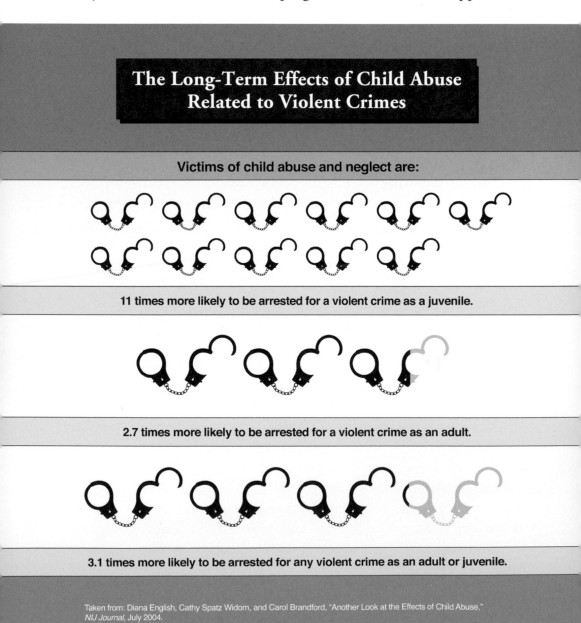

The Long-Term Effects of Child Abuse Related to Violent Crimes

Victims of child abuse and neglect are:

11 times more likely to be arrested for a violent crime as a juvenile.

2.7 times more likely to be arrested for a violent crime as an adult.

3.1 times more likely to be arrested for any violent crime as an adult or juvenile.

Taken from: Diana English, Cathy Spatz Widom, and Carol Brandford, "Another Look at the Effects of Child Abuse," *NIJ Journal*, July 2004.

can prevent child maltreatment in high-risk families, with programs longer than two years having the strongest effects.

Nevertheless, not all home visitation programs have demonstrated positive impacts for all populations in preventing child maltreatment or improving parental capacity. The recent research does point to a need to better address the needs of families with the highest risk factors for child maltreatment such as those with caregivers with problems associated with mental health, substance abuse, and domestic violence. Some of the studies indicated that home visiting may be most effective for families where the initial need is the greatest and where parents are motivated to change and seek assistance. Other reviews also point to the importance of maintaining fidelity to the original model and the need for well-trained and well-supervised home visitors who can implement the original program as intended in order to produce positive impacts for families served.

Research has shown that home visitation, by trained nurses, in programs with strong performance monitoring and management systems, can reduce incidents of child abuse and neglect and improve other life outcomes for mothers and their children. In a well-known, randomized, longitudinal research trial, outcomes from one nurse home visitation program showed a nearly 80 percent reduction in rate of child maltreatment among at-risk families from birth through children's 15th year. Other research has shown that nurse home visits had a long-term positive effect on other family outcomes, such as reduced substance abuse, reduced arrests and convictions, greater work-force participation, reduced reliance on public assistance and food stamps, and reduced early sexual activity on the part of the children visited.

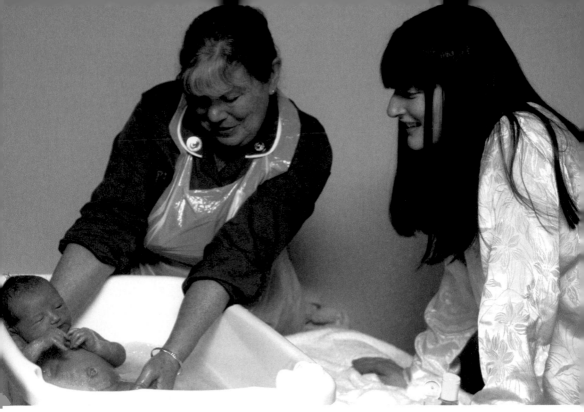

There are now programs available in which nurses or other professionals come into homes and teach basic parenting skills to young parents.

Finally, there is a limited but emerging body of research using randomized controlled trials on other home visitation models that also have had positive impacts on child abuse and neglect and other related outcomes such as promoting the increase in protective factors and decreasing risk factors for children and caregivers served.

EVALUATING THE AUTHORS' ARGUMENTS:

In this viewpoint Maiso Bryant focuses on in-home visitation. Compare her position with the preceding selection by Francie Zimmerman and James A. Mercy, which deals with treating child maltreatment as a public health concern. What are the strengths and weaknesses of each approach? Explain your answer using evidence from each viewpoint.

The US Child Protection System Works to Safeguard Children

John E.B. Myers

> *"The child protection system protects children every hour of the day."*

Law professor John E.B. Myers is a nationally recognized author and expert on child abuse and neglect. In the following viewpoint Myers discusses the history of the US child protection system. He says that organized governmental efforts to protect children from abuse and neglect in the United States did not begin until 1962. Prior to this, only nongovernmental groups were concerned about child protection. Myers says that the US child protection system is not perfect, but it is not a failure either. The lives of countless numbers of children have been saved because of the US child protection system, he claims.

AS YOU READ, CONSIDER THE FOLLOWING QUESTIONS:
  1. What was the name of the article that Myers says was pivotal in bringing attention to child abuse in 1962, and who is its author?
  2. According to the author, in what year did all fifty states have child abuse reporting laws for the first time?
  3. What does Myers say is the name of the federal child protection law passed in 1974?

The history of child protection in America is divisible into three eras. The first era extends from colonial times to 1875 and may be referred to as the era before organized child protection. The second era spans 1875 to 1962 and witnessed the creation and growth of organized child protection through nongovernmental child protection societies. The year 1962 marks the beginning of the third or modern era: the era of government-sponsored child protective services. . . .

Child Abuse Becomes a National Issue

The 1960s witnessed an explosion of interest in child abuse, and physicians played a key role in this awakening. Prior to the 1960s, medical schools provided little or no training on child abuse, and medical texts were largely silent on the issue. Even pediatricians were largely uninformed. The spark that eventually ignited medical interest in abuse was an article published in 1946 by pediatric radiologist John Caffey. Caffey described six young children with subdural hematoma and fractures of the legs or arms. Although Caffey did not state that any of the children were abused, he hinted at it. Following Caffey's classic paper, a small but steady stream of physicians drew attention to the abusive origin of some childhood injuries. This trend culminated in the 1962 publication of the blockbuster article "The Battered Child Syndrome" by pediatrician Henry Kempe and his colleagues. Kempe played a leading role in bringing child abuse to national attention during the 1960s and 1970s.

As the medical profession became interested in child abuse, so did the media. Local media had always covered noteworthy cases, as when a child was beaten to death, but coverage by national media was uncommon prior to the 1960s. Following publication of *The Battered Child Syndrome*, national news outlets like *Newsweek, Saturday Evening Post, Parents Magazine, Time, Good Housekeeping*, and *Life* published emotional stories of abuse, often citing *The Battered Child Syndrome* and Henry Kempe. A *Newsweek* story from April 1962, for example, was titled "When They're Angry" and quoted Kempe: "One day last November, we had four battered children in our pediatrics ward. Two died in the hospital and one died at home four weeks later. For every child who enters the hospital this badly beaten, there must be hundreds treated by unsuspecting doctors. The battered child syndrome isn't a reportable disease, but it damn well ought to be."

The Role of Media and Legislation

Prior to 1962, there was little professional research and writing about abuse. [Social worker] Elizabeth Elmer noted, "The amount of systematic research on the problem of abuse and neglect is conspicuously scant." Following publication of *The Battered Child Syndrome*, a trickle of writing became a torrent that continues to this day.

News stories and journal articles captured public and professional attention. Behind the scenes, Congress placed new emphasis on child protection with amendments to the Social Security Act in 1962. Vincent De Francis [director of the Children's Division of the Charitable American Humane Association] remarked that the 1962 amendments "for the first time, identified Child Protective Services as part of all public child welfare." In addition to sharpening the focus on child protection, the 1962 amendments required states to pledge that by July 1, 1975, they would make child welfare services available statewide. This requirement fueled expansion of government child-welfare services, including protective services.

Child Maltreatment: States with Highest Victimization Rates

These rates are based on the numbers of child abuse and neglect victims per 1,000 children from October 1, 2007, through September 30, 2008. The national rate for the fiscal year 2008 is 10.3.

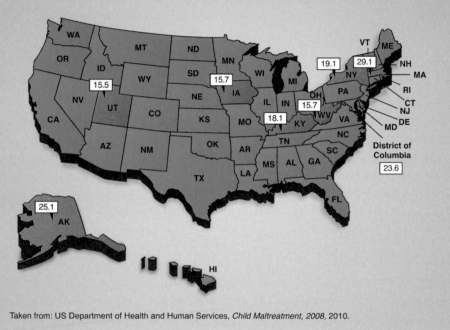

Taken from: US Department of Health and Human Services, *Child Maltreatment, 2008*, 2010.

The year 1962 was momentous not only for publication of *The Battered Child Syndrome* and amendments to the Social Security Act. In the same year, the federal Children's Bureau convened two meetings to determine how the Bureau could more effectively help states respond to child abuse. Attendees at the meetings, including Henry Kempe and Vincent De Francis, recommended state legislation requiring doctors to report suspicions of abuse to police or child welfare. These meetings were the genesis of child abuse reporting laws, the first four of which were enacted in 1963. By 1967, all states had reporting laws.

Reporting the Problems and Finding Solutions

As reporting laws went into effect, the prevalence of child abuse and neglect came into focus. By 1974, some 60,000 cases were reported.

In 1980, the number exceeded one million. By 1990, reports topped two million, and in 2000, reports hovered around three million. In the early twenty-first century, reports declined but remained high.

Turning from reporting laws to another critical component of child protection, foster care, during the nineteenth century, children who could not live safely at home ended up in orphanages or almshouses. Nineteenth-century reformers like Charles Loring Brace struggled to remove children from institutions and place them in foster homes. Debate over the merits of foster care versus orphanage care raged from the 1850s to the early decades of the twentieth century. Eventually, proponents of foster care prevailed, and almshouses and orphanages disappeared.

In the early days, foster care was viewed as a major advance and as the best solution for many dependent children. In the last quarter of the twentieth century, however, some came to view foster care as a problem rather than as a solution. Critics lamented that nearly half a million children are in foster care at any point in time and that too many children get "stuck" in out-of-home care. What's more, children of color, particularly African-American children, are sadly overrepresented among foster children. Yet, despite problems, foster care remains a safe haven for many abused and neglected children.

The Federal Government Assumes a Leadership Role

Prior to 1974, the federal government played a useful but minor role in child protection. The Children's Bureau was founded in 1912, but the Bureau paid little attention to maltreatment until the 1960s. The Social Security Act of 1935, as amended in 1962, provided money to expand child welfare services. Yet, as late as 1973, U.S. Senator Walter Mondale wrote, "Nowhere in the Federal Government could we find one official assigned full time to the prevention, identification and treatment of child abuse and neglect."

Due in substantial measure to Mondale's efforts, Congress assumed a leadership role with passage of the Child Abuse Prevention and Treatment Act of 1974 (CAPTA). CAPTA authorized federal funds to improve the state response to physical abuse, neglect, and sexual abuse. CAPTA focused particular attention on improved investigation and reporting. In addition, CAPTA provided funds for training, for regional multidisciplinary centers focused on child abuse and

Minnesota senator Walter Mondale was the driving force behind the Child Abuse Prevention and Treatment Act of 1974 (CAPTA). CAPTA authorized the use of federal funds to improve states' responses to child abuse and neglect.

neglect, and for demonstration projects. Responsibility for administering CAPTA was placed in a new agency, the National Center on Child Abuse and Neglect. The Center funded important research on maltreatment. CAPTA played a major role in shaping the nationwide system of governmental child protective services in place today. In addition, CAPTA marked the final passing of privately funded, nongovernmental child protection societies. Congress periodically renewed CAPTA, and this important legislation remains in force today. . . .

The System Saves Lives and Futures

Forty years ago [around 1968], child protection pioneer Vincent De Francis lamented, "No state and no community has developed a Child Protective Service program adequate in size to meet the service needs of all reported cases of child neglect, abuse and exploitation." What would De Francis say today? I believe he would say that although today's child protection system has many problems, the contemporary system is a vast improvement over the incomplete patchwork that existed in the 1960s. Today, child protective services are available across America, billions of dollars are devoted to child welfare, and thousands of professionals do their best to help struggling parents and vulnerable children.

The child protection system protects children every hour of the day. Unfortunately, the public seldom hears about child protection's successes. Indeed, the only time child protection makes the front page or the evening news is when something goes terribly wrong: social workers fail to remove an endangered child who ends up dead, or social workers remove children when they should not. Both scenarios—over- and under-intervention—are inevitable in the difficult work of child protection. Yet, the fact that the public hears only about child protection's failings undermines confidence in the system. The truth is that the system saves lives and futures. As you read this sentence, a social worker somewhere is making a decision that will protect a child. As we look back across history, it is clear that the effort to protect children is not a story of failure, but a story of progress and hope. The child protection system is far from perfect, and much remains to he done, but, at the same time, much has been accomplished.

EVALUATING THE AUTHOR'S ARGUMENTS:

Do you think John E.B. Myers's discussion of the history of child protection provides an effective way to make his case that the US child protection system is a success? Why, or why not?

Viewpoint
4

The US Child Protection System Does Not Work

"Evidence shows that Child Protective Services . . . is a broken system not merely full of cracks, but riddled with big gaping holes that America's children are falling into."

Lisa Nixon

Child protective service (CPS) agencies in the United States are failing to protect children, contends Lisa Nixon in the following viewpoint. According to Nixon, statistics show that more children die when CPS is involved than when it is not. Yet, nothing is ever done, she says, and CPS workers are never held accountable for their failures. She believes the child protection system in the United States must be changed before more children die. Nixon has a degree in paralegal technologies. She writes about child abuse for the online news source *Examiner.com*.

AS YOU READ, CONSIDER THE FOLLOWING QUESTIONS:

1. According to Nixon, the report by the organization Every Child Matters contains a list of children who died between 2001 and 2009. How many children are on the list?
2. According to the author, child protection directors and social workers hide behind what two kinds of laws?
3. What does Nixon say is the only way to stop the needless deaths of children such as Kayla Allen?

Lisa Nixon, "America's Dead Children and Child Protection Services," *Examiner.com*, November 12, 2009. Reproduced by permission.

T he list is long and heartbreaking, the children on it have been beaten, broken, drowned, burned, strangled, starved or neglected, and all of them are dead. Headlines have drawn attention to the cases of some of them, Danieal Kelly, Erin Maxwell, Kayla Allen, and Christopher Thomas, but there are many more, Phoenix Jordan Cody-Parrish, Brandon Williams, Elizabeth Goodwin, Logan Marr and Alexis (Lexie) Agyepong-Grover, just to name a few.

The children on this list died in very different settings; some died in their own homes, some in foster care, while others were killed by their adoptive parents. Yet, all of these dead, abused, children had one thing in common, Child Protective Services [CPS].

Statistics Point to CPS Responsibility

[Activist] Bill Bowen in his short documentary film, *Innocents Destroyed*, states that, "Over 1,000 children die of neglect or are tortured and murdered each year, in the care of an entity where children are up to 600% more likely to die a horrific death, CPS."

According to Child Welfare Information Gateway [a government service], "The National Child Abuse and Neglect Data System (NCANDS) reported an estimated 1,760 child fatalities in 2007." All of these deaths are attributed to child abuse or neglect.

The math of these statistics is alarming, if these numbers are to be believed roughly 57% of all child abuse deaths in America have some type of Child Protective Services involvement.

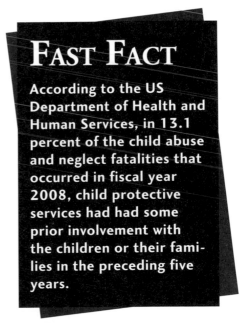

FAST FACT

According to the US Department of Health and Human Services, in 13.1 percent of the child abuse and neglect fatalities that occurred in fiscal year 2008, child protective services had had some prior involvement with the children or their families in the preceding five years.

In a report released by Every Child Matters, titled, "We Can Do Better," there is a list of 51 children that died between 2001 and

2009. During research on the children listed in this report, this reporter found the following:

- 27 of them (53% percent) had prior Child Protective Services involvement before their deaths
- 19 had no evidence or no evidence was found of prior CPS involvement
- 4 had previous investigations or convictions for child abuse on children other than their victim, 1 of these had a report of abuse made to the police and 1 was a known sex offender
- 1 was a police officer who killed his girlfriend's child

The numbers are eye opening; more children are dying in this country with CPS involvement than without it.

No Accountability

The pattern of these types of deaths has become the norm in this country. A child dies of abuse or neglect and then it is later discovered that CPS was already involved with the family, that the child was a foster child, or had been adopted by the parent who killed them. CPS is rarely held accountable in these cases, even when negligence is proven; there is no punishment for the agencies that are legally obligated to perform the duties of Child Protection.

The directors and social workers in these cases hide behind confidentiality laws, that were initially implemented to protect families and children, but that now seem merely in place to protect CPS. They also hide behind immunity laws that make it nearly impossible for them to be held accountable for these children's deaths.

Criminal prosecution for these workers is almost unheard of, even with proof of forged documents, perjury, failure to perform statutory duties, and in some cases a complete and total disregard for the well being of the children entrusted to their care. These workers, their supervisors, and all involved walk away from these deaths free and clear without any ramifications for their behavior at all, often-times right back into the office and back to work, like nothing ever happened.

It is hard to get a District Attorney or the Police to investigate the people they work so closely with on a daily basis, who they may even consider friends.

When Negligence Becomes Obstruction of Child Protection

Take for example the North Carolina death of Kayla Allen. Onslow County had received numerous reports of abuse on Kayla, they even received pictures of bruises on Kayla taken by the Michigan Police Department after Kayla's grandmother out of desperation to protect Kayla from the blatant abuse that was being ignored by Onslow County, kidnapped Kayla and took her home to Michigan.

Kayla's grandmother was arrested, and Kayla was returned to North Carolina into the care of Carolyn Furtell. Kayla would be dead 14 months later and Carolyn Furtell was eventually convicted of involuntary manslaughter in her death. Kayla's grandmother committed

Child-care provider Carolyn Furtell was convicted of involuntary manslaughter in the death of seven-year-old Kayla Allen.

suicide after Kayla's death because she had promised her beloved granddaughter that no one would ever hurt her again.

The Onslow County Department of Social Services [DSS] was not held accountable for their failure to protect Kayla; in fact, Roger Penrod, Onslow County Director of Social Services stated, "I've reviewed the case, and no one has found any fault in what DSS was involved in," he said. "That doesn't satisfy some people. They are free to say what they want, but I can't comment on it." . . .

How to End These Needless Deaths

The needless deaths of these children have to stop and the only way to do that is to change the laws that govern Child Protective Services.

- In this country when someone breaks the law, whether it is a police officer, a doctor, or an ordinary citizen, they are charged with a crime. Should it be any different for CPS?
- When a doctor is negligent in performing his duties and his patient is injured or killed because of that negligence he is held accountable. Should it be any different for CPS?
- When a child dies, and there is even the suspicion that the other parent could have known of the abuse, that parent is charged with failure to protect. Should it be any different for CPS?
- When a government agency in this country isn't following the law and performing its duties as required, they are investigated, and if needed, the Federal Government intervenes to make them perform those duties or shuts them down. Should it be any different for CPS?

Evidence shows that Child Protective Services isn't working in this country; it is a broken system not merely full of cracks, but riddled with big gaping holes that America's children are falling into. Hasn't the time come to change this department?

Complaints about Child Protective Services at the federal level are met with the assertion that CPS is not a federal issue, but a state issue. How can that be when children in every state are dying with Child Protective Services involvement? Children dying in America are not just a state issue, it is a national issue and until these American children's deaths are viewed as an American problem, the deaths will continue.

EVALUATING THE AUTHORS' ARGUMENTS:

Compare and contrast Lisa Nixon's viewpoint with that of the previous selection by John E.B. Myers. Whose viewpoint do you think is stronger, and why? Support your answer with examples from the text.

Spanking Should Be Banned

Alan E. Kazdin

> *"More than one-third of all parents who start out with relatively mild punishments end up crossing the line drawn by the state to define child abuse."*

In the following viewpoint, Alan E. Kazdin argues that the United States should consider banning spanking, or corporal punishment, in the home. According to Kazdin, there are many scientific and moral reasons that should deter parents from using corporal punishment. For instance, Kazdin says that one-third of all parents who spank their kids end up breaking child abuse laws. He argues that the United States should ban spanking in schools and in homes as many other countries already do. Kazdin is a psychology professor at Yale University. He has authored many child psychology books, including the 2009 book *The Kazdin Method for Parenting the Defiant Child.*

AS YOU READ, CONSIDER THE FOLLOWING QUESTIONS:

1. What percentage of American parents does Kazdin say physically discipline their one- to two-year-old children?
2. According to Kazdin, how many states ban corporal punishment in schools?

3. What is the name of the United Nations agreement that specifies that governments must take appropriate measures to protect
children from all forms of physical or mental violence, injury or
abuse, neglect or negligent treatment, maltreatment or exploitation? Has the United States ratified this agreement?

The typical parent, when whacking a misbehaving child, doesn't pause to wonder: "What does science have to say about the efficacy of corporal punishment?" If they are thinking anything at all, it's: "Here comes justice!" And while the typical parent may not know or care, the science on corporal punishment of kids is pretty clear. Despite the rise of the timeout and other nonphysical forms of punishment, most American parents hit, pinch, shake, or otherwise lay violent hands on their youngsters: 63 percent of parents physically discipline their 1- to 2-year-olds, and 85 percent of adolescents have been physically punished by their parents. Parents cite children's aggression and failure to comply with a request as the most common reasons for hitting them.

Corporal Punishment Is Addictive

The science also shows that corporal punishment is like smoking: It's a rare human being who can refrain from stepping up from a mild, relatively harmless dose to an excessive and harmful one. Three cigarettes a month won't hurt you much, and a little smack on the behind once a month won't harm your child. But who smokes three cigarettes a month? To call corporal punishment addictive would be imprecise, but there's a strong natural tendency to escalate the frequency and severity of punishment. More than one-third of all parents who start out with relatively mild punishments end up crossing the line drawn by the state to define child abuse: hitting with an object, harsh and cruel hitting, and so on. Children, endowed with wonderful flexibility and ability to learn, typically adapt to punishment faster than parents can escalate it, which helps encourage a little hitting to lead to a lot of hitting. And, like frequent smoking, frequent corporal punishment has serious, well-proven bad effects.

Studies have shown that in one-third of parents who start out spanking their children, their disciplinary methods will escalate to those meeting the legal definition of child abuse.

The negative effects on children include increased aggression and noncompliance—the very misbehaviors that most often inspire parents to hit in the first place—as well as poor academic achievement, poor quality of parent-child relationships, and increased risk of a mental-health problem (depression or anxiety, for instance). High levels of corporal punishment are also associated with problems that crop up later in life, including diminished ability to control one's impulses and poor physical-health outcomes (cancer, heart disease, chronic respiratory disease). Plus, there's the effect of increasing parents' aggression, and don't forget the consistent finding that physical punishment is a weak strategy for permanently changing behavior.

Why Parents Hit Their Kids

But parents keep on hitting. Why? The key is corporal punishment's temporary effectiveness in stopping a behavior. It does work—for a moment, anyway. The direct experience of that momentary pause in misbehavior has a powerful effect, conditioning the parent to hit again next time to achieve that jolt of fleeting success and blinding the parent to the long-term failure of hitting to improve behavior. The research consistently shows that the unwanted behavior will return at the same rate as before. But parents believe that corporal punishment works, and they are further encouraged in that belief by feeling that they have a right and even a duty to punish as harshly as necessary.

Part of the problem is that most of us pay, at best, selective attention to science—and scientists, for their part, have not done a good job of publicizing what they know about corporal punishment. Studies of parents have demonstrated that if they are predisposed not to see a problem in the way they rear their children, then they tend to dismiss any scientific finding suggesting that this presumed nonproblem is, in fact, a problem. In other words, if parents believe that hitting is an effective way to control children's behavior, and especially if that conviction is backed up by a strong moral, religious, or other cultural rationale for corporal punishment, they will confidently throw out any scientific findings that don't comport with their sense of their own experience.

FAST FACT

According to an ABC News poll conducted in October of 2002, "The public, by a 2 to 1 margin, approves of spanking children in principle, and half of parents say they sometimes do it to their own kids."

The catch is that we frequently misperceive our own experience. Studies of parents' perceptions of child rearing, in particular, show

Based on statistical analysis of mothers' responses in an anonymous phone survey conducted in North and South Carolina in 2002, 12 percent of mothers who reported spanking fifty times in the last year also reported abuse.

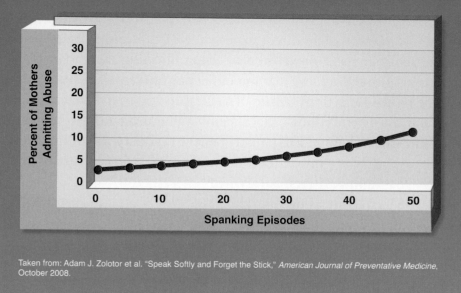

Taken from: Adam J. Zolotor et al. "Speak Softly and Forget the Stick," *American Journal of Preventative Medicine,* October 2008.

that memory is an extremely unreliable guide in judging the efficacy of punishment. Those who believe in corporal punishment tend to remember that hitting a child worked: She talked back to me, I slapped her face, she shut her mouth. But they tend to forget that, after the brief pause brought on by having her face slapped, the child talked back again, and the talking back grew nastier and more frequent over time as the slaps grew harder.

The Arguments Against Hitting Children

So what's the case for not hitting? It can be argued from the science: Physical discipline doesn't work over the long run, it has bad side effects, and mild punishment often becomes more severe over time. Opponents of corporal punishment also advance moral and legal arguments. If you hit another adult you can be arrested and sued, after all, so shouldn't our smallest, weakest citizens have a right to equal or even more-than-equal protection under the law? In this country, if you do the same thing to your dog that you do to your child, you're more likely to get in trouble for mistreating the dog.

The combination of scientific and moral/legal arguments has been effective in debates about discipline in public schools. Twenty-eight states and the District of Columbia have banned corporal punishment in the schools. But so far, we have shown ourselves unwilling to extend that debate beyond the schools and into the ideologically sacred circle of the family. Where the argument against corporal punishment in the schools has prevailed, in fact, it has often cited parents' individual right to punish their own children as they, and not educators acting for the state, see fit. The situation is different in other countries. You may not be surprised to hear that 91 countries have banned corporal punishment in the schools, but you may be surprised to hear that 23 countries have banned corporal punishment everywhere within their borders, including in the home.

I know what you're thinking: Are there really 23 Scandinavian countries? Sweden was, indeed, the first to pass a comprehensive ban, but the list also includes Hungary, Bulgaria, Spain, Israel, Portugal, Greece, Uruguay, Chile, Venezuela, and New Zealand. According to advocates of the ban, another 20 or so countries are committed to full prohibition and/or are debating prohibitionist bills in parliament. The Council of Europe was the first intergovernmental body to launch a campaign for universal prohibition across its 47 member countries.

The United Nations' Prohibition on
Violence Against Children

Practically nobody in America knows or cares that the United Nations has set a target date of 2009 for a universal prohibition of violence against children that would include a ban on corporal punishment in the home. Americans no doubt have many reasons—some of them quite good—to ignore or laugh off instructions from the United Nations on how to raise their kids. And it's naive to think that comprehensive bans are comprehensively effective. Kids still get hit in every country on earth. But especially because such bans are usually promoted with large public campaigns of education and opinion-shaping (similar to successful efforts in this country to change attitudes toward littering and smoking), they do have measurable good effects. So far, the results suggest that after the ban is passed, parents hit less and are less favorably inclined toward physical discipline, and the country is not overwhelmed by a wave of brattiness and delinquency. The opposite, in fact. If anything, the results tell us that there's less deviant child behavior.

There could conceivably be good reasons for Americans to decide, after careful consideration, that our commitment to the privacy and individual rights of parents is too strong to allow for an enforceable comprehensive ban on corporal punishment. But we don't seem to be ready to join much of the rest of the world in even having a serious discussion about such a ban. In the overheated climate of nondebate encouraged by those who would have us believe that we are embroiled in an ongoing high-stakes culture war, we mostly just declaim our fixed opinions at one another.

One result of this standoff is that the United States, despite being one of the primary authors of the U.N.'s Convention on the Rights of Children, which specifies that governments must take appropriate measures to protect children from "all forms of physical or mental violence, injury or abuse, neglect or negligent treatment, maltreatment or exploitation," is one of only two nations that have not ratified it. The other is Somalia; 192 nations have ratified it. According to my colleague Liz Gershoff of the University of Michigan, a leading expert on corporal punishment of children, the main arguments that have so far prevented us from ratifying it include the ones you would expect—it would undermine American parents' authority as well as U.S. sovereignty—plus a couple of others that you might not have expected: It would not allow 17-year-olds to enlist in the armed forces, and (although the Supreme Court's decision in *Roper v. Simmons* has made this one moot, at least for now) it would not allow executions of people who committed capital crimes when they were under 18.

Time for a Debate in the United States

We have so far limited our national debate on corporal punishment by focusing it on the schools and conducting it at the local and state levels. We have shied away from even theoretically questioning the primacy of rights that parents exercise in the home, where most of the hitting takes place. Whatever one's position on corporal punishment, we ought to be able to at least discuss it with each other like grownups.

EVALUATING THE AUTHOR'S ARGUMENTS:

According to Alan E. Kazdin, there are scientific, moral, and legal reasons that parents should not hit their children. Which of these types of reasoning does he primarily use to support his viewpoint? Provide specific examples from the text.

Spanking Should Not Be Banned

"The empirical data indicate that a spanking ban is a grave mistake. With spanking bans have come increased rates of child abuse."

Jason M. Fuller

In the following viewpoint Jason M. Fuller contends that spanking bans are more harmful than they are beneficial. According to Fuller, many people think spanking bans will make society less violent. However, the opposite is true. Both child abuse and youth violence increase after the enactment of a spanking ban, says Fuller. He wants more people to hear about the benefits of spanking. Fuller is a law student at the University of Akron in Akron, Ohio.

AS YOU READ, CONSIDER THE FOLLOWING QUESTIONS:

1. According to Fuller, which two US states introduced legislation to ban spanking in 2007?
2. According to the author, which European country's supreme court said the following when enacting a spanking ban: "Correction of children" was both "culturally anachronistic and historically outdated"?
3. Fuller says that on average, spanking seems to reduce aggression, defiance, and antisocial behavior better than what other types of punishment?

In 2005, a group of thirteen-year-old Swedish boys began terrorizing a family by threatening to kill the family's son, forcing the mother's car off the road and ripping open her rear door, publicly humiliating them, damaging and stealing their property, emptying and sabotaging their mailbox, brandishing planks at them, and surrounding them with weapons. Over the next two years, the harassment became so intolerable that the father shot at the group of teens, killing one.

Were such a killing to occur in the U.S., the popular reaction would have been, "How can we prevent this from happening again?" In Sweden, however, youth violence and aggression has gotten so out-of-control that the reaction was, "Shoot another [one]." Sadly, many policymakers fail to realize how Swedish laws have contributed to growing youth violence, and consequently, to public resentment of Swedish youths.

The Trend to Ban Spanking

In 1979, Sweden started an international trend by becoming the first country to ban spanking. Since then, twenty-three more countries have outlawed it. The European Committee of Social Rights currently is urging all forty-five of its member nations to ban corporal punishment. In 2007 alone, the Netherlands, New Zealand, Portugal, Uruguay, Venezuela, Spain, and Chile each enacted laws forbidding parents from using physical discipline. In that same year, California and Massachusetts also introduced legislation to ban spanking.

Anti-spanking laws are proposed and passed with the hope that they will create a "cultural spillover" of non-violence, and a society that does not need correction. For instance, when Italy's Supreme Court declared spanking unlawful, it said the very expression "correction of children" was both "culturally anachronistic and historically outdated."

> **FAST FACT**
>
> According to the Child Trends Databank in 2004, 79 percent of women aged eighteen to twenty-four and 61 percent of women aged forty-five to sixty-five agreed that it is sometimes necessary to give a child a "good hard spanking."

Parents Today Spank and Yell Less than Their Own Parents Did

The data below is drawn from an office-based survey of 2,134 parents bringing children, aged two to eleven, for a well-child examination in thirty-two states, Puerto Rico, and Canada. The survey asked about discipline in the past month, as well as how the parents themselves had been disciplined when they were children.

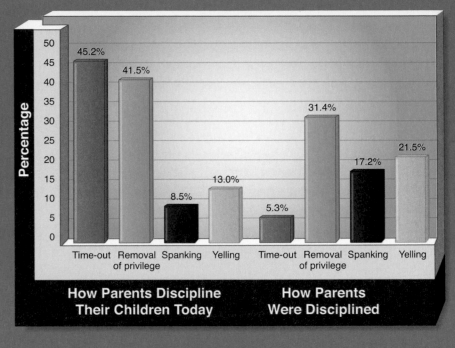

Taken from: Shari Barkin et al. "Determinants of Parental Discipline Practices: A National Sample from Primary Care Practices," *Clinical Pediatrics*, January 2007.

While such lawmaking may seem harmless, even commendable, the empirical data indicate that a spanking ban is a grave mistake. With spanking bans have come increased rates of child abuse, aggressive parenting, and youth violence. Indeed, criminal records suggest that children raised under a spanking ban are much more likely to be involved in crime than other children.

This makes sense. To function well in society, children need to learn that misbehavior has negative consequences. But not every child learns this the same way. If one child learns best about misbehav-

122   **Child Abuse**

ior through physical punishment, he should receive a spanking. If another learns this best through mental punishment, she should get a timeout. To keep any helpful discipline method from a child may restrict his ability to mature, and could make him an unnecessary burden on society.

The author maintains that spanking reduces some forms of antisocial behavior, and many parents believe that the practice is more helpful than harmful.

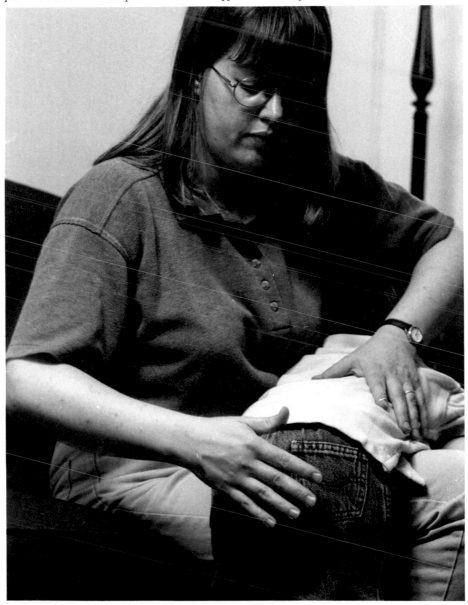

Spanking Is Not Harmful

Yet many people want to deprive children of spanking, even though the most sound research suggests it is not harmful, and is often more helpful than other common discipline methods. On average, spanking seems to reduce aggression, defiance, and antisocial behavior better than mental punishments like timeout, reasoning, privilege removal, threats, verbal power assertion, ignoring, love withdrawal, or diverting.

Nevertheless, spanking's successes are largely ignored. Many philosophically oppose corporal punishment and praise spanking bans, but few honestly consider the entire body of child discipline statistics. Therefore, in this rapidly changing area of the law that lies at the heart of our children's education and future, only one side of the story is being told. . . . And if we continue to ignore [the other] side, our children may be the ones that suffer.

EVALUATING THE AUTHORS' ARGUMENTS:

In the selection you have just read, Jason M. Fuller argues that spanking bans are harmful to children and to society. In the previous viewpoint Alan E. Kazdin contends that spanking is a harmful and ineffective punishment. After reading both viewpoints, what is your opinion on spanking and spanking bans? Cite from both texts to support your argument.

Facts About Child Abuse

According to Childhelp.org,
- A report of child abuse is made every ten seconds.
- Almost five children die every day as a result of child abuse. More than three out of four are under the age of 4.
- It is estimated that between 60 and 85 percent of child fatalities due to maltreatment are not recorded as such on death certificates.
- Ninety percent of child sexual abuse victims know the perpetrator in some way; 68 percent are abused by family members.
- Child abuse occurs at every socioeconomic level, across ethnic and cultural lines, within all religions, and at all levels of education.

According to the US Centers for Disease Control and Prevention (CDC):
- In 2008 US state and local child protective services (CPS) received 3.3 million reports of children being abused or neglected.
- CPS estimated that 772,000 (10.3 per 1,000) children were victims of maltreatment.
- In 2008 one in five American children experienced some form of child maltreatment: approximately 1 percent were victims of sexual assault; 4 percent were victims of child neglect; 9 percent were victims of physical abuse; and 12 percent were victims of emotional abuse.
- In 2008 71 percent of maltreated children were classified as victims of child neglect; 16 percent as victims of physical abuse; 9 percent as victims of sexual abuse; and 7 percent as victims of emotional abuse.
- In 2008 CPS reported the approximate rates of child maltreatment victims:
    - 21.7 per 1,000 for infants less than 1 year old;
    - 12.9 per 1,000 for 1-year-olds;
    - 12.4 per 1,000 for 2-year-olds;
    - 11.7 per 1,000 for 3-year-olds;
    - 11.0 per 1,000 for 4- to 7-year-olds;
    - 9.2 per 1,000 for 8- to 11-year-olds;
    - 8.4 per 1,000 for 12- to 15-year-olds; and
    - 5.5 per 1,000 for 16- to 17-year-olds.

- In 2008 some children had higher rates of victimization:
  - African American (16.6 per 1,000 children);
  - American Indian or Alaska Native (13.9 per 1,000 children);
  - Multiracial (13.8 per 1,000 children);
  - Overall, rates of victimization were slightly higher for girls (10.8 per 1,000 children) than boys (9.7 per 1,000 children).

Facts About Child Abuse Perpetrators

According to the CDC:
- Most children are maltreated by their parents versus other relatives or caregivers.
- Perpetrators are typically less than 39 years of age.
- Female perpetrators, mostly mothers, are typically younger than male perpetrators.

Facts About Child Abuse Deaths

According to the CDC:
- In 2008 an estimated 1,740 children aged 0 to 17 died from abuse and neglect (rate of 2.3 per 100,000 children).
  - 80 percent of deaths occurred among children younger than age 4;
  - 10 percent among 4- to 7-year-olds;
  - 4 percent among 8- to 11-year-olds;
  - 4 percent among 12- to 15-year-olds; and
  - 2 percent among 16- to 17-year-olds.
  - 39 percent of deaths were non-Hispanic white children.
  - 30 percent of deaths were African American children.
  - 16 percent of deaths were Hispanic children.

Facts About Child Abuse and Criminal Behavior

According to Childhelp.org:
- Thirty-six percent of all women and 14 percent of all men in prison in the United States were abused as children.
- Children who experience child abuse and neglect are 59 percent more likely to be arrested as juveniles, 28 percent more likely to be arrested as adults, and 30 percent more likely to commit violent crimes.

Facts About Child Abuse Consequences

According to Childhelp.org:
- Abused children are 25 percent more likely to experience teen pregnancy.

- Abused teens are 3 times less likely to practice safe sex, putting them at greater risk for sexually transmitted infections (STIs).
- About 30 percent of abused and neglected children will later abuse their own children, continuing the cycle of abuse.
- About 80 percent of 21-year-olds abused as children meet criteria for at least one psychological disorder.

Facts About Child Abuse and Substance Abuse

According to Childhelp.org:
- Children who have been sexually abused are 2.5 times more likely to abuse alcohol.
- Children who have been sexually abused are 3.8 times more likely to develop drug addictions.
- Nearly two-thirds of the people in treatment for drug abuse report being abused as children.

Facts About Child Abuse Around the World

According to UNICEF (United Nations Children's Fund), an estimated 300 million children worldwide are subjected to violence, exploitation, and abuse. This treatment includes the worst forms of child labor in communities, schools, and institutions; abuse during armed conflict; and harmful practices such as female genital mutilation/cutting and child marriage.

According to the World Health Organization:
- It is estimated that 5.7 million children are trapped into forced or bonded labor.
- An estimated 14 million adolescents between 15 and 19 give birth each year.
- According to the latest estimates for 2002, some 1.2 million children are trafficked worldwide every year.
- Estimates suggest that more than 250,000 children are currently serving as child soldiers.
- An estimated 133 million children are orphans (children aged 0 to 17 who have lost one or both parents) worldwide.
- It is estimated that more than 130 million women and girls alive today have been subjected to female genital mutilation/cutting.
- Studies conducted since 1980 suggest that worldwide 20 percent of women and 5 to 10 percent of men suffered sexual abuse as children.

- In a cross-sectional survey of children in Egypt, 37 percent reported being beaten or tied up by their parents and 26 percent reported physical injuries such as fractures, loss of consciousness, or permanent disability as a result of being beaten or tied up.
- In a survey in the Republic of Korea, two-thirds of parents reported whipping their children and 45 percent confirmed that they had hit, kicked, or beaten them.
- A survey of households in Romania found that 4.6 percent of children reported suffering severe and frequent physical abuse, including being hit with an object, being burned, or being deprived of food. Nearly half of Romanian parents admitted to beating their children "regularly" and 16 percent to beating their children with objects.
- In Ethiopia, 21 percent of urban schoolchildren and 64 percent of rural schoolchildren reported bruises or swelling on their bodies resulting from parental punishment.

Organizations to Contact

The editors have compiled the following list of organizations concerned with the issues debated in this book. The descriptions are derived from materials provided by the organizations. All have publications or information available for interested readers. The list was compiled on the date of publication of the present volume; the information provided here may change. Be aware that many organizations take several weeks or longer to respond to inquiries, so allow as much time as possible for the receipt of requested materials.

Administration for Children and Families (ACF)

370 L'Enfant Promenade SW, Washington, DC 20447
website: www.acf.hhs.gov

The ACF is an agency within the US Department of Health and Human Services. The ACF is responsible for federal programs that promote the economic and social well-being of families, children, individuals, and communities. The Offices of Child Care and of Child Support Enforcement are primarily responsible for child abuse prevention in collaboration with other ACF offices. The ACF's Child Welfare Information Gateway provides many child abuse and neglect prevention resources.

American Humane Association

63 Inverness Dr. East, Englewood, CO 80112
(800) 227-4645 or (303) 792-9900
fax: (303) 792-5333
e-mail: info@americanhumane.org
website: www.americanhumane.org

The mission of the American Humane Association is to create a more humane and compassionate world by ending abuse and neglect of children and animals. As the nation's voice for the protection of children and animals, the American Humane Association reaches millions of people every day through groundbreaking research, education, training, and services that span a wide network of organizations, agencies, and businesses. The organization's quarterly journal, *Protecting Children*, provides information on a variety of child welfare topics.

American Professional Society on the Abuse of Children (APSAC)
350 Poplar Ave., Elmhurst, IL 60126
(630) 941-1235 or (877) 402-7722
fax: (630) 359-4274
e-mail: apsac@apsac.org
website: www.apsac.org

APSAC is a nonprofit national organization focused on meeting the needs of professionals engaged in all aspects of services for maltreated children and their families. Especially important to APSAC is the dissemination of state-of-the-art practice in all professional disciplines related to child abuse and neglect. APSAC publishes two quarterly journals, the *APSAC Child Maltreatment Journal* and the *APSAC Advisor.* Additionally, every year or so the organization publishes the *APSAC Handbook on Child Maltreatment.*

Annie E. Casey Foundation
701 St. Paul St., Baltimore, MD 21202
(410) 547-6600
fax: (410) 547-6624
e-mail: webmail@aecf.org
website: www.aecf.org

The Annie E. Casey Foundation is a private charitable organization dedicated to helping provide a better future for disadvantaged children in the United States. The primary mission of the foundation is to foster public policies, human-service reforms, and community supports that more effectively meet the needs of today's vulnerable children and families. In pursuit of this goal, the foundation makes grants that help states, cities, and neighborhoods fashion more innovative, cost-effective responses to these needs. The foundation provides many publications, including the monthly magazine *Urbanite* and the annual statistical report *Kids Count Data Book.*

Childhelp
15757 N. Seventy-Eighth St., Ste. B, Scottsdale, AZ 85260
(480) 922-8212
fax: (480) 922-7061
e-mail: nationaldayofhope@childhelp.org
website: www.childhelp.org

Childhelp is a national nonprofit organization dedicated to helping victims of child abuse and neglect. Childhelp focuses on prevention, intervention, and treatment. The organization provides residential treatment services and child abuse prevention, education, and training. Additionally, Childhelp operates children's advocacy centers, therapeutic foster care, group homes, and a national child abuse hotline. Childhelp was instrumental in the federal government's recognition of April as National Child Abuse Prevention Month and in the establishment of the National Day of Hope.

Children's Defense Fund (CDF)

25 E St. NW, Washington, DC 20001
(202) 628-8787
fax: (800) 233-1200
e-mail: cdfinfo@childrensdefense.org
website: www.childrensdefense.org

The CDF is a nonprofit child advocacy organization that champions policies and programs that lift children out of poverty, protect them from abuse and neglect, and ensure their access to health care, quality education, and a moral and spiritual foundation. The organization issues a monthly *eNewsletter* that provides an update on CDF's efforts on behalf of children, information on the issues affecting America's children, and tips on how people can take action on these issues.

Every Child Matters Education Fund

2000 M St. NW, Ste. 203, Washington, DC 20036
(202) 223-8177
fax: (202) 223-8499
e-mail: info@everychildmatters.org
website: www.everychildmatters.org

The Every Child Matters Education Fund is a national nonprofit organization working to make children, youth, and families a national political priority. Preventing child abuse is one of the focus areas of Every Child Matters. The group seeks to educate policy makers and the public and to provide information to prevent violence against children in their homes and communities. It also works to ensure that children have access to health care, to expand early learning opportunities, and to alleviate child poverty. The organization's annual report on child abuse deaths, *We Can Do Better: Child Abuse Deaths in America,* provides statistics on child abuse deaths in America.

International Society for Prevention of Child Abuse and Neglect (ISPCAN)
13123 E. Sixteenth Ave., B390, Aurora, CO 80045-7106
(303) 864-5220
fax: (303) 864-5222
e-mail: ispcan@ispcan.org
website: www.ispcan.org

ISPCAN is an international organization that works to prevent cruelty to children in every nation and in every form, including physical abuse, sexual abuse, emotional abuse, neglect, street children, child fatalities, child prostitution, children of war, and child labor. ISPCAN seeks to increase awareness of the extent, the causes, and the possible solutions for all forms of child abuse; to disseminate research to those in positions to enhance practice and improve policy; to support international efforts to promote and protect the rights of the child; and to improve the quality of current efforts to detect, treat, and prevent child abuse. The organization's publications include the monthly journal *Child Abuse and Neglect: The International Journal*, as well as *World Perspectives on Child Abuse*. These publications provide an overview of the state of child maltreatment policy and practice in over seventy countries.

National Council on Child Abuse and Family Violence (NCCAFV)
1025 Connecticut Ave. NW, Ste. 1000, Washington, DC 20036
(202) 429-6695
fax: (202) 521-3479
e-mail: info@nccafv.org
website: www.nccafv.org

The NCCAFV provides prevention services by bringing together community and national stakeholders, volunteers, and professionals to prevent intergenerational family violence, including child abuse and neglect, spouse/partner abuse, and elder abuse and neglect. The American Campaign for Prevention of Child Abuse and Family Violence is the organization's latest prevention effort. *In Forum* is the organization's electronic newsletter.

Prevent Child Abuse America
228 S. Wabash Ave., 10th Fl., Chicago, IL 60604
(312) 663-3520
fax: (312) 939-8962

e-mail: mailbox@preventchildabuse.org
website: www.preventchildabuse.org

The mission of Prevent Child Abuse America is to prevent all forms of abuse and neglect directed toward children, including physical, sexual, educational, and emotional abuse and neglect. The organization advocates for public policies that diminish or eliminate the risk factors for child abuse, and promotes protective policies. Prevent Child Abuse America's publications include *Great Beginnings, STAGES, Pocket Guides to Parenting Series, Marvel Comics' Amazing Spider-Man Series* and several others.

UNICEF
United States Fund for UNICEF, 125 Maiden Lane, 11th Fl., New York, NY 10038
(212) 686-5522
fax: (212) 779-1679
e-mail: www.unicefusa.org/about/contact
website: www.unicef.org

UNICEF, or the United Nations Children's Fund, works in 190 countries around the world as it seeks to overcome the obstacles that poverty, violence, disease, and discrimination place in a child's path. Child protection is one of UNICEF's core missions. The organization advocates and supports the creation of a protective environment for children by supporting national child protection systems, protective social practices, as well as oversight and monitoring. UNICEF offers myriad publications for child protection professionals and the public, including its annual *The State of the World's Children.*

Voice of the Faithful (VOTF)
PO Box 423, Newton Upper Falls, MA 02464
(781) 559-3360
fax: (781) 559-3364
e-mail: office@votf.org
website: http://votf.org

The VOTF was formed in 2002 by lay members of the Catholic Church in response to the clergy sexual abuse scandals. The organization's goals are to support survivors of clergy sexual abuse, support priests of integrity, and to shape structural change within the Catholic Church. Among its activities, the VOTF actively seeks to support the formation and activities of Child Abuse Prevention teams in every Catholic parish. The organization's publications include *In the Vineyard* and *Focus.*

For Further Reading

Books

Clark, Robin E., Judith Freeman Clark, and Christine Adamec. *The Encyclopedia of Child Abuse*. New York: Facts On File, 2007. In this reference book concerning child abuse, the authors discuss the characteristics and causes of abuse, its impact on children, various types of abuse, treatments for both the abused and the abuser, and other social and legal issues surrounding the topic.

Crosson-Tower, Cynthia. *Understanding Child Abuse and Neglect*. Boston: Allyn & Bacon, 2010. This text offers a comprehensive look at child maltreatment, including a history of child welfare, case studies, and her own experience as a child protection worker. The author also provides a discussion of ways to prevent child abuse.

Einhorn, Lois. *Forgiveness and Child Abuse: Would You Forgive?* Bandon, OR: Robert D. Reed, 2010. The author, a professor of communications at the State University of New York, recounts the years she spent being tormented by an abusive mother and then asks more than fifty prominent people whether they would forgive such treatment. Their answers are provided in this book, which serves to encourage discussion and debate about child abuse and to move readers from fear and revenge to love and forgiveness.

Feerick, Margaret Mary. *Child Abuse and Neglect*. Baltimore: Paul H. Brookes, 2006. This text examines the history of classification and identification of child abuse, provides suggestions for future research, and gives researchers an overview of how policy trends and practice can advance or impede progress in this area.

Finkelhor, David. *Child Victimization*. New York: Oxford University Press, 2008. This renowned expert presents a comprehensive new concept of "developmental victimology" to encompass the prevention, treatment, and study of juvenile victims, unifying conventional subdivisions like child molestation, child abuse, bullying, and exposure to community violence. The author looks at child victimization across childhood's span and provides insights about how to categorize juvenile victimizations, how to think about risk and impact, and how victimization patterns change over the course of development.

Gerrits, Julie. *Child Abuse.* New York: Crabtree, 2010. The author, a child psychologist, examines the issues of child maltreatment, including physical, emotional, and sexual abuse and neglect. She discusses disclosure and feeling safe and explains how abuse and neglect affect children and adults.

McCoy, Monica L., and Stefanie M. Keen. *Child Abuse and Neglect.* Florence, KY: Psychology, 2009. The authors provide a history of child maltreatment through the years, as well as the latest research and risk factors for child abuse. Many topics are explored, including mandated reporting and different forms of maltreatment.

Pelzer, David J. *A Child Called "It": One Child's Courage to Survive.* Deerfield Beach, FL: Health Communications, 1995. The author provides a horrifying memoir of the torment he endured as a young child at the hands of his mother. He was starved, stabbed, smashed face-first into mirrors, forced to eat unspeakable items, and burned over a gas stove by his alcoholic mother. Saved by a schoolteacher, he survived his torment and went on to write this and many other books.

Philpot, Terry. *Understanding Child Abuse: The Partners of Child Sex Offenders Tell Their Stories.* New York: Routledge, 2009. The author presents a voice for women whose partners have sexually abused children. The women, many of whom were victims of child sexual abuse themselves, tell their stories, how they feel about the situations in which they found themselves, how they coped, and how they remade their lives and those of their families.

Richardson, Tom I., and Marsha V. Williams, eds., *Child Abuse and Violence.* New York: Nova Biomedical, 2008. Social workers, psychologists, and others discuss and debate many child abuse topics in this book. Child abuse perpetrated by adolescent mothers, incest, and child abuse in Japan are among the topics discussed by the contributors.

Roesler, Thomas A., and Carole Jenny. *Medical Child Abuse: Beyond Munchausen Syndrome by Proxy.* Elk Grove Village, IL: American Academy of Pediatrics, 2009. Roesler, a child psychiatrist, and Jenny, a pediatrician, discuss where medical child abuse stands in the overall landscape of child abuse. The authors make the case that the term *Munchausen syndrome by proxy*—in which an adult caregiver, usually the mother, makes a child sick by either fabricating symptoms or actually causing harm to the child—should be retired permanently and replaced with a commonsense understanding that parents can medically abuse their children in a number of ways.

Smith, Margaret G., and Rowena Fong. *The Children of Neglect: When No One Cares*. New York: Routledge, 2004. The authors provide a comprehensive review of child neglect, an often over-looked form of child maltreatment. Included are statistics, defini-tional issues, policy issues, and an examination of the relationship of child neglect to poverty, substance abuse, and culture.

Staller, Karen M., and Kathleen Coulborn Faller. *Seeking Justice in Child Sexual Abuse: Shifting Burdens and Sharing Responsibilities*. New York: Columbia University Press, 2010. The authors analyze one rural community's unique approach to handling accusations of child sexual abuse. Hoping to spare children the trauma of testify-ing in court, professionals in a small community in the midwest United States, strive to obtain confessions from accused sex offend-ers rather than asking the victim to bear the burden.

Turton, Jackie. *Child Abuse, Gender, and Society*. New York: Routledge, 2008. Turton examines the behavior of female as well as male perpetrators of child sexual abuse. The book includes case studies and insights from professionals in the field.

Vieth, Victor, Bette L. Bottoms, and Alison R. Perona. *Ending Child Abuse*. Florence, KY: Psychology, 2005. This book is a collection of essays about child abuse prevention strategies written by social scien-tists and legal scholars. According to the contributors, several obstacles stand in the way of the elimination of child abuse, such as the failure to investigate most child abuse reports, inadequate training of front-line child protection professionals, lack of financial resources, and the dilemma that child abuse is not addressed at the youngest ages.

Periodicals

Asheville (NC) Citizen Times. "Child Abuse Deaths Demand Closer Attention," December 22, 2010.

Bialik, Carl. "New Research on Spanking Might Need a Time Out," *Wall Street Journal,* October 14, 2009.

Crary, David. "Abuse Risk Seen Worse as Families Change," *USA Today,* November 19, 2009.

DeGregory, Lane. "The Girl in the Window," *St. Petersburg (FL) Times,* July 31, 2008.

Floyd, Jacquielynn. "The Truth About Child Abuse Cannot Be Ignored," *Dallas Morning News,* December 22, 2010.

Garcia, Mary Jane. "Let's Step Up Child Abuse Prevention," *Albuquerque Journal,* July 11, 2010.

Gonnerman, Jennifer. "School of Shock," *Mother Jones,* September/October 2007.

Greenhut, Steven. "Child Abuse by the Government," *Orange County (CA) Register,* February 17, 2008.

Hession, Gregory. "This Is Child Protection?," *New American,* July 23, 2007.

Hewitt, Bill. "Little Girl Lost," *People,* April 11, 2008.

Keegan, Roseann. "A Mother's Story," *Tahoe Daily Tribune* (South Lake Tahoe, CA), December 22, 2010.

Keegan, Roseann. "State of Nevada Below Standard for Tracking Child Abuse," *Carson City Nevada Appeal,* December 20, 2010.

Lewis, Nancy. "Child Abuse and Neglect Cases Decline, Deaths Rise," *Youth Today,* December 20, 2010.

Lowenstein, Jeff Kelly. "Safe at Home?," *Chicago Reporter,* November/December 2010.

Medical News Today. "Child Abuse Causes Lifelong Changes to DNA Expression and Brain," February 23, 2009.

Paul, Pamela. "Is Spanking OK?," *Time,* May 8, 2006.

Paxson Christina, and Ron Haskins. "Introducing the Issue," *Preventing Child Maltreatment,* Fall 2009.

Pediatrics Week. "Unemployment Linked with Child Maltreatment," October 23, 2010.

Sandoval, Tammy. "Parents Are Key to Curbing Child Abuse," *Anchorage Daily News,* April 16, 2008.

Skenazy, Lenore. "America's Worst Mom," *New York Sun*, April 8, 2008.

Spears, Ronald. "Humpty Dumpty Child," *Illinois Bar Journal*, November 2010.

Stafford, Wess. "A Candle in the Darkness," *Christianity Today*, May 2010.

Thompson, Richard, and Jiyoung K. Tabone. "The Impact of Early Alleged Maltreatment on Behavioral Trajectories," *Child Abuse & Neglect*, December 2010.

Wachter, Kerri. "Childhood Abuse Linked to Type 2 Diabetes in Women," *Family Practice News*, November 15, 2010.

Weigel, George. "What Went Wrong," *Newsweek*, April 12, 2010.

Websites

American Academy of Child & Adolescent Psychiatry (http://aacap.org/cs/root/facts_for_families/facts_for_families). This website's Facts for Families page provides concise and up-to-date information on issues that affect children, teenagers, and their families.

Child Trauma Academy (www.childtrauma.org). The Child Trauma Academy is a not-for-profit organization based in Houston, Texas, that works to improve the lives of high-risk children through direct service, research, and education.

Child Welfare Information Gateway (www.childwelfare.gov). This website operated by the US Administration for Children and Families provides access to information and resources to help protect children and strengthen families.

Crimes Against Children Research Center (www.unh.edu/ccrc). The Crimes Against Children Research Center provides research and statistics to the public, law enforcement personnel, and policy makers about the nature of crimes such as child abduction, homicide, rape, assault, and physical and sexual abuse, as well as their impacts.

Kempe Foundation for the Prevention and Treatment of Child Abuse and Neglect (www.kempe.org). Provides information, resources, and stories about child abuse and child abuse prevention.

National Council on Child Abuse and Family Violence (NCCAFV) (www.nccafv.org). The NCCAFV's website provides information to assist, inform, and link child abuse and family violence victims with those individuals and agencies that can help them.

We Can Do Better—Child Abuse Deaths in America (http://www .everychildmatters.org/storage/documents/pdf/reports/wcdbv2 .pdf). An annual report from the Every Child Matters Education Fund provides statistics on child abuse deaths in America.

Index

A

AAP (American Academy of Pediatrics), 7–8
Abel, Gene, 75
Adverse Child Experiences Study (ACE), 91
AIHW (Australian Institute of Health and Welfare), 56, 57
Aleccia, JoNel, 39
Allen, Kayla, 109–110
American Academy of Pediatrics (AAP), 7–8
American Psychiatric Association (APA), 76
APA (American Psychiatric Association), 76
Archives of Sexual Behavior (journal), 76
Arizona Review (newsletter), 10
Australian Institute of Criminology, 56
Australian Institute of Health and Welfare (AIHW), 56, 57

B

Batmanghelidjh, Camila, 30–31
The Battered Child Syndrome (Kempe *et al.*), 100, 101, 102
Behavior Today (journal), 76
Benedict XVI (pope), 24, *25*
Berger, Rachel, 46, 48
BJS (Bureau of Justice Statistics), 34, 35, 37
Blankenhorn, David, 59

Bowen, Bill, 107
Brace, Charles Loring, 103
Brown, Andrew, 27
Brown, Nixzmary, *58*
Bryant, Maiso, 94
Burdekin, Brian, 56
Bureau of Justice Statistics, US (BJS), 34, 35, 37
Bush, George W., *35*

C

Caffey, John, 100
Califia, Pat, 76
CAPTA (Child Abuse Prevention and Treatment Act, 1974), 103–104
Catholic Church
  child sexual abuse in, is no worse in than in rest of world, 27–31
  child sexual abuse is a crisis in, 22–26
  costs of clergy sex abuse to, 28
CDC (Centers for Disease Control and Prevention), 14
Center for the Study of Social Policy, 93
Centers for Disease Control and Prevention (CDC), 14
Chicago Longitudinal Study, 93
Child abuse
  association between spanking and, *116*
  consequences of, 89–91, 97

does not cause child sexual abuse, 79–84
Human Rights Watch, 37

I
Innocents Destroyed (film), 107
Isaac, Troy Erik, 33

J
Jenny, Carole, 46
Joltes, Richard E., 60
Jones, Lisa, 49
Journal of Pediatrics, 40
Journal of Sex Research, 76
Juvenile prisons
    child sexual abuse is epidemic in, 32–38
    percent of youth forced to have sex with staff in, 33

K
Kaiser, David, 32
Kazdin, Alan E., 112
Kempe, Henry, 100, 101
Kinsey, Alfred, 75
Kort, Joe, 79
Kramer, Larry, 76

L
Leave It to Beaver (TV program), 62, *63*
Lombard, Frank, 75
Luther, Martin, 23

M
Martin, Diarmuid, *30*
Mercy, James A., 86
Miletski, Hani, 84
Mondale, Walter, 103, *104*

Mother-Son Incest (Miletski), 84
Mothers
    correlation between spanking and abuse by, *116*
    percentage of child abuse/ neglect victims mistreated by, 64
    on spanking/abuse, *116*
Muehlenberg, Bill, 54
Myers, John E.B., 99

N
National Catholic Reporter (newspaper), 23
National Child Abuse and Neglect Data System (NCANDS), 50–51, 52, 107
National Child Abuse Prevention Month, 13
National Committee to Prevent Child Abuse, 69
National Incidence Study of Child Abuse and Neglect (NIS-4), 17, 18, 51–52, 75
National Prison Rape Elimination Commission, 35
National Survey of Children's Exposure to Violence (NatSCEV), 89
NCANDS (National Child Abuse and Neglect Data System), 50–51, 52, 107
Newton, Alice, 48
"Ninety-five Theses on the Power and Efficacy of Indulgences" (Luther), 23
NIS-4 (National Incidence Study of Child Abuse and Neglect), 17, 18, 51–52, 75

Nixon, Lisa, 106
Nurse Family Partnership
    Program, 14

O
The Observer (newspaper), 8
Opinion polls. *See* Surveys
L'Osservatore Romano
    (newspaper), 25

P
Parent education programs,
    in-home, can help prevent child
    abuse, 94–98
Parents
    biological, children are safest
        with, 55–56
    methods of discipline used by
        vs. received by, *122*
    responsible for child
        maltreatment, by parental
        type, *61*
Paterson, David, 38
Pedophilia, definition of, 80
Pleasantville (film), 62
Poisoning/poisoning deaths
    of children under age five,
        reasons for, *43*
    links to physical abuse, 42–43
    prevalence of, 40
Polls. *See* Surveys
Positive Parenting Program, 14
Poverty, as factor in child abuse,
    48
PREA (Prison Rape Elimination
    Act, 2003), 34, *35*
*Predators, Pedophiles, Rapists and
    other Sex Offenders* (Salter), *82*
Prevent Child Abuse America,

13–14, 69
Prevent Child Abuse New York,
    91
Prevention/prevention programs,
    14–16
    federal government takes
        leadership role in, 103
    in-home parent education
        programs are effective in,
        94–98
    public health approach to,
        86–93
Prison Rape Elimination Act
    (PREA, 2003), 34, *35*

R
Race/ethnicity, living
    arrangements of children by,
    57
Ratzinger, Georg, 28
Ratzinger, Joseph. *See* Benedict
    XVI
Recession
    is linked to decrease in child
        abuse cases, 49–53
    is linked to increase in child
        abuse cases, 45–48
Reid, Jane, 70
Rizal, Ardi, 7
Roper v. Simmons (2005), 118

S
Salter, Anna C., 82
San Francisco Sentinel
    (newspaper), 76
Schapira, David, 10
Scribano, Philip, 46
Secondhand smoke, 7–8
Sedlak, Andrea, 21

Picture Credits

ABC/The Kobal Collection, 63

© Angela Hampton Picture Library/Alamy, 98

AP Images/Daily News, 109

AP Images/Henry Griffin, 104

AP Images/Ben Margot, 41

AP Images/PRNewsFoto/Emerald Coast Children's Advocacy Center, 85

AP Images/Allessandra Tarantino, 25

AP Images/Winslow Townson, 88

Mark C. Burnett/Photo Researchers, Inc., 13

Niall Carson/PA Photos/Landov, 30

Mauro Fermariello/Photo Researchers, Inc, 11, 114

Gale, a part of Cengage Learning, 15, 19, 29, 36, 43, 52, 57, 61, 72, 83, 90, 96, 102, 116, 122

Landov, 20

Ursula Markus/Photo Researchers, Inc., 47

Spencer Platt/Getty Images, 58

Réunion des Musées Nationaux / Art Resource, NY, 77

Rob Schoenbaum/Time Life Pictures/Getty Images, 123

© Ian Thraves/Alamy, 70

Jim Varney/Photo Researchers, Inc, 44

© Cal Vornberger/Alamy, 81

White House/HO/Landov, 35